Paddy Hopkirk says:

'Sooner or later, every car owner faces the
ruinous cost of servicing, maintaining and
repairing his car. That's why more and
more car owners are turning to DIY methods
as the only way of slashing motoring costs.

PITMAN'S ALL-IN-ONE motoring books are
written by professional motoring writers
who understand car owners' needs.
The books have been specially designed to
give all the information needed, in clear
diagrams, trouble-shooting charts, photo-
graphs and easy-to-follow text, making it
easy for DIY car owners to keep costs of
motoring at rock bottom.

Whatever the car owner's approach to home
servicing - whether as a novice or an expert
- PITMAN'S ALL-IN-ONE motoring books offer
him for the first time a combined maintenance handbook and workshop manual - all the
DIY car owner needs to get the best out of
his car.'

Paddy Hopkirk

A late version of the 12 TS. Automatic-transmission cars share many details of the external and internal trim and equipment with this model.

The Renault 12 saloon. This is a pre-1976 model, identifiable by the vertical air-extraction grille behind the rear door.

The roomy Renault 12 estate. The folding rear seat provides a very large carrying capacity without sacrificing comfort.

All-in-one
book of the
Renault 12

Staton Abbey

A maintenance,
fault-tracing and home
workshop manual

Covering Renault 12
synchromesh-gearbox and
automatic-transmission models
R1170 — L, TL
R1171 — TN estate
R1177 — TR, TS, Auto
R1330 — TL, TN estate
R1337 — TR, TS estate

Pitman

Pitman Publishing Ltd
39 Parker Street, London WC2B 5PB

Associated Companies

Copp Clark Ltd, Toronto
Fearon-Pitman Publishers Inc, Belmont, California
Pitman Publishing Co SA (Pty) Ltd, Johannesburg
Pitman Publishing New Zealand Ltd, Wellington
Pitman Publishing Pty Ltd, Melbourne

© Staton Abbey 1977

ISBN 0 273 01070 0

Designed and illustrated by Collis, Inglis, Smith
Set in Univers light by Wordsworth Typesetting
Printed in England by the Pitman Press, Bath

Contents

Part one

1 **Before you begin —**   7
How this series was planned

2 **Getting to know your car —**   8
Facts and figures

3 **Vetting a used car —**   10
How to detect or forestall trouble

4 **Planned servicing —**   12
Preventive maintenance

Part two

5 **Trouble-shooting —**   17
6 **Bodywork defects —**   30
7 **The Ministry test—**   33

Part three

8 **Strip, repair or replace? —**   35
Practical notes on overhauls

9 **The engine**   37
10 **The cooling system**   54
11 **The carburettor and petrol pump**   59
12 **The ignition system**   63
13 **The transmission —**   69
Clutch, gearbox, propeller shaft, rear axle

14 **The suspension and steering**   79
15 **The braking system**   86
16 **The electrical system**   96
17 **Specifications and overhaul data**   104
   Metric conversion tables   109
   Index   111

Acknowledgements

Special thanks are due to Renault Ltd for providing information and advice during the preparation of this book, and also to the parent company at Billancourt in France for permission to use drawings in the official workshop manuals as the basis of many of the illustrations

Among other firms to whom thanks are due are –

Champion Sparking Plug Company Ltd
AE Edmunds Walker Ltd
Holt Products Ltd

The greatest care has been taken to check and cross-check the information and servicing data, but liability cannot be accepted for errors or omissions, or for changes in specifications that are sometimes introduced by a manufacturer during the production run of a model

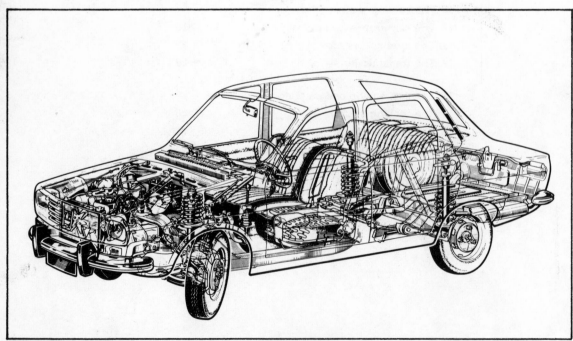

This partly-sectioned drawing of a Renault 12 saloon is typical of the range. Although a left-hand-drive model is shown, the right-hand-drive cars are similar in general layout.

Part one

1 Before you begin
How this series was planned

Are you a dedicated do-it-yourself enthusiast – or an owner with only limited practical experience, forced by continually rising costs to maintain and repair your car at home?

Whatever your approach to home servicing – whether as a novice or as an expert – the handbooks in this series have been tailored to meet your needs and abilities. Each forms a combined, all-in-one maintenance handbook and home workshop manual, with the emphasis solidly on the practical aspects of the work.

We introduce you to your car, advise you how to vet a used example, tell you how to get it through the Ministry test and take you progressively through preventive maintenance, trouble-shooting, servicing, repairs and overhauls.

We have made the workshop manual chapters as comprehensive as possible, while bearing in mind the less than ideal conditions under which the average owner must usually carry out repairs and overhauls. But it must be accepted that some jobs are outside the province of the home mechanic; they call for the use of special workshop tools and equipment and – in many cases – for special skills.

Botched-up repairs can be dangerous and we feel strongly that owners should not be encouraged to do work which might entail safety risks.

How this book is arranged

In Part One you will find an in-depth study of the models covered, together with information on servicing and preventive maintenance. We take the logical view that it is better to avoid trouble than to try to put it right after it has developed.

Even the most meticulous maintenance, however, cannot guarantee freedom from faults, so we have included in Part Two a comprehensive set of trouble-tracing charts which should enable you to pin-point a trouble quickly and accurately.

If your car is due for the Ministry test, the tips that we give should enable it to pass with flying colours. Many cars fail quite unnecessarily, due to faults which could have been put right by a practical owner.

While still on the theme of putting your car in tip-top condition, we tell you how to tackle rust and bodywork blemishes and how to restore a showroom shine.

The remainder of the book forms a concise home workshop manual, covering all the jobs that can be safely tackled without the need for elaborate equipment, and supported by comprehensive specifications and data tables.

The practical aspects

We have tried to anticipate your difficulties and to give practical pointers and advice where necessary. For example, would it be quicker and cheaper to fit a new or fully-reconditioned part instead of stripping and repairing a worn component? When should the help of a specialist repair firm be enlisted? We give you the pros and cons (and the economics) of these problems, to help you to make the correct decision.

Time is often a vital factor and we have included in the workshop manual chapters what we think are some realistic times for the more important jobs and major operations. We have erred on the generous side, bearing in mind the needs of the novice, but it would be wise to allow an additional safety margin to take care of unexpected snags. The times that we suggest, therefore, will not necessarily agree with those that may be quoted by a dealer, who has a well-equipped workshop and racks full of expensive special tools.

Finally, we have broken down the servicing and overhaul instructions into simple step-by-step sequences which are exceptionally easy to follow and should give a beginner the confidence to tackle fairly ambitious work.

Where there are snags, we don't hesitate to say so. And where special service tools and other equipment are needed, we list them.

As for the work itself, that is – literally – in your hands. We hope that we shall have helped to make it a little easier.

2 Getting to know your car
Facts and figures

Take a typically French combination of extremely comfortable seating and soft but well-damped suspension. Add lively performance and very good steering and roadholding. Combine these desirable features with a modest fuel consumption, and you will go a long way towards explaining the excellent press reviews which the Renault 12 L and TL versions received when they were introduced at the Paris show in the autumn of 1969.

The cars met with an equally enthusiastic reception when they were launched in the UK in May 1970 and owners soon found that even the basic 12 could more than hold its own, in terms of performance and quiet high-speed cruising, with competitive 1300 cc models.

The 12 TS, however — the *Tourisme Speciale*, launched in the UK in October 1972 — with its more highly-tuned engine, twin-choke Weber carburettor, rev counter, sports-type wheels and other additional equipment, had an even greater appeal to the enthusiast.

Owners who required greater carrying capacity were catered for by the estate car, which first reached the UK in 1971, and for those who valued the ease of driving conferred by an automatic gearbox the 12 TR — later termed the 12 Auto — was introduced in the Spring of 1974.

Renault service literature uses reference numbers, such as R1170, R1171, R1177 and R1330 to distinguish the various models whereas owners usually refer to their cars simply as 12 L, TL, TS or estate versions, but the chart in Chapter 17 will help to sort out the differences between the various specifications.

The cars which are available in the UK are described in this and later chapters. It has not been possible, in the space available, to include the many variants which are exported, assembled or built under licence in other countries.

Incidentally there is another point which must be borne in mind: car design is never static, and modifications are often made during the production run of a particular model, which may affect some of the details listed. If in doubt, you will usually find your Renault dealer ready to give friendly advice.

The engine

All models are fitted with 1298 cc overhead-valve engines, with the valves operated by short push-rods. In standard tune these engines are quiet and reliable, but produce only a modest power output of 54 bhp DIN at 5250 rpm.

As already mentioned, however, in the Autumn of 1972 an additional model, the 12 TS, was introduced in the UK. The TS engine has a more sporting camshaft and a Weber twin-choke carburettor. These raise the power to 60 bhp at 5500 rpm and give the car a much more lively performance and a top speed of over 95 mph.

All the engines have die-cast light-alloy cylinder heads and crankcases, with 'wet' cylinder liners. This construction means that if gasket troubles and cylinder-head distortion are to be prevented, particular care is needed when fitting and removing the cylinder head and regular checks must be made on the tightness of the cylinder-head bolts.

Nevertheless, when properly looked after the engines are not temperamental, even in the more highly-tuned TS form, and are capable of running for 60 000-80 000 miles between overhauls.

An excellent feature of the design is that matched sets of new pistons and cylinder barrels can be installed, and the connecting-rod bearings and oil pump can be renewed, without removing the engine from the car.

The transmission

Unlike the arrangement used with other Renault front-wheel-drive models, the four-speed synchromesh gearbox or the optional automatic transmission, together with the final-drive gears and the drive shafts, are mounted behind the engine. The gearbox is controlled through a remote-control linkage which is precise in action but not as light as we have come to expect from some competitors.

Renault automatic transmissions have a good reputation for reliability, and the electronic control system seems to be free from gremlins. Upward changes are notably smooth; downward changes less so, chiefly because there is no part-throttle down-change facility, automatic downward changes being made only at fairly wide throttle openings.

The suspension and steering

Coil springs at front and rear give very soft suspension with a long wheel travel that ensures an extremely good ride, plus the ability to soak-up rough surfaces and potholes without the need to slacken speed — the suspension, in fact, is typically French.

Also typically French is the tendency to allow considerable initial roll when cornering fast. This can be disconcerting at first — especially to a passenger — but one soon realizes that once the car has taken up its initial roll angle it is immensely stable and the ability of the soft springs to keep all four wheels on the ground results in exceptionally good roadholding.

With the engine mounted ahead of the gearbox, the car is nose-heavy and therefore tends to understeer strongly, or run wide, when cornering. The steering, however, is light, even at parking speeds, and one soon comes to terms with the understeer, which does have the advantage of giving excellent straight-line stability at speed.

The brakes

The braking system is a conventional front disc/rear drum set-up, with vacuum-servo assistance on the TS and on the later estate and TL models. When in good condition the brakes give good retardation for modest pedal pressure. A limiting valve in the rear brake line controls the maximum pressure which can be exerted in the rear brake cylinders according to the load carried and thus helps to prevent premature locking of the rear wheels. In 1972 the rather unsatisfactory handbrake lever was removed from the dash and a much more convenient lever fitted between the front seats. The earlier arrangement is, however, quite adequate as a parking brake.

Model line-up

Now for a brief summary of the most important changes and new models that have been introduced in the UK since May 1970.

1970, May. L and TL four-door saloon models introduced in UK. L model had a bench-type front seat, TL model separate, reclining seats and more luxurious equipment. Both cars had front-wheel-drive, a 1289 cc engine mounted ahead of a four-speed all-synchromesh gearbox, disc front/drum rear brakes and an alternator as standard.

1970, September. Improved equipment for L and TL models included heated rear window (optional extra on L), front passenger grab handle, matt-black radiator grille surround and stainless steel strips beneath the doors and boot lid.

1971, January. Estate car (12 TN) launched in UK. Based on saloon mechanical parts but with stronger rear springs, larger-diameter rear-brake drums and thicker anti-roll bar.

1971, September. Repeater flashers no longer fitted to front wings. Carpet fitted to driving compartment of TL. Heated rear window available as an optional extra on estate car.

1972, August. Handbrake removed from dash and fitted between front seats. Combined armrest and door-pull fitted to TL. Mileage trip recorder and illuminated windscreen-wiper button on both models. Servo-assisted brakes on estate car.

1972, October. 12 TS model introduced in UK. Engine, fitted with twin-choke Weber carburettor and sporting camshaft, develops 68 bhp. Improved equipment included sports-type wheels with 155-15 section tyres, rev counter, high-backed reclining front seats, servo brakes, heated rear window as standard. Specification otherwise similar to TL model.

1973, August. All models wired to allow reversing lamps to be fitted. TS cars had modified headlamps with long-range quartz-iodine beams (so-called 'kangaroo' headlamps because extra bulb was incorporated in each reflector). Heated rear window now standard on estate car.

1974, April. 12 TR automatic model introduced in UK. Specification same as TL, but with engine to TS specification and TS-type high-backed front seats. Three-speed automatic gearbox controlled by electronic computer. Windscreen wash-wipe facility.

1974, August. L and estate car models fitted with dipping rear-view mirrors. Estate car had windscreen wash-wipe facility and also adjustment for height of headlamp from driver's compartment.

1975, October. All models given a major face-lift which included restyled radiator grille, heavier, wrap-around bumpers incorporating side-lights and flashers at the front, new rectangular rear-light cluster, and horizontal instead of vertical air-extraction grilles on rear quarters. Fascia redesigned. All models fitted with windscreen wash-wipe facility, controlled by steering column stalk. 12 TL estate no longer termed TN and automatic version now called 12 Auto, not 12 TR. 12 TL saloon now had brake servo, bringing it into line with the TL estate. Mechanical changes included higher compression ratio and carburettor emission-control modifications for TL and TL estate. These engines require four-star fuel but 12 L with original 8.5:1 compression ratio will run on three-star fuel.

Typical average performance figures

Maximum speed in gears — mph

	1st	2nd	3rd	Top
12 L, TL	30	45	70	88
12TS	30	50	75	94
12 TR, Auto	Low, 42	Inter, 68	Top, 88	

Acceleration — 30-50 mph in top gear

12 L, TL	12.5 seconds	12 TR, Auto	7 seconds (kick down)
12 TS	12 seconds	12 estate	14 seconds

Fuel consumption

12 L, TL	28-35 mpg
12 TS	26-35 mpg
12 TR, Auto	26-33 mpg

3 Vetting a used car
How to detect or forestall trouble

Many used-car dealers tend to fight shy of the majority of 'foreign' cars when considering a part-exchange deal, but they will usually accept a well-maintained Renault 12 quite happily. This is, perhaps, the best evidence that these cars have proved to be very reliable in service and free from potentially expensive troubles.

Buying any used car, however, must always be something of a gamble, so it will pay to carry out a really thorough check on all the points mentioned in this chapter before concluding the deal. If you have already bought a used model, give it a similar vetting before deciding what work will be needed to put it in really good condition.

As each check is completed, fill-in a detailed inspection record (see page 18). The time will be well repaid later when summing-up the overall condition of the car and planning the work to be done.

Begin with the bodywork

A used car that is more than one or two years old should be carefully checked for rust. As any car salesman knows, repair of badly corroded areas can be expensive. Fortunately Renault 12 models are given a very thorough treatment with Tectyl — a well-known anti-rust preparation — during manufacture and have an above-average resistance to rust in service, even under adverse conditions.

The most vulnerable spots seem to be along the bottoms of the doors and at the spot-welded flange where the sills join the floorpan. In the latter case, however, cleaning off the rust with a wire brush and applying a coat of zinc-rich paint, followed by normal retouching, should be all that is needed to cure the trouble. The rust here seldom poses a structural problem.

Make sure that any rust which has developed due to stones chipping the paintwork behind the rear wheels has not developed beyond surface corrosion. Again, restoring the finish should be within the scope of any practical owner.

At some stage during the inspection it is best to have the vehicle raised on a lift, if possible, or at least on wheel ramps or on axle stands, so that the underbody can be carefully inspected.

Apart from checking for rust, also pay special attention to the safety points mentioned on page 12.

Checking engine condition

Renault engines have long lives. Properly looked after, a used example should not need any major attention before it has covered about 60 000-80 000 miles — and then, as indicated in Chapters 8 and 9, essential repairs should be well within the scope of a practical owner, with a certain amount of help from specialist firms.

During a road test you should expect to find the engine very sweet and smooth, except for a characteristic vibration which comes in at around 2500-3000 rpm (approximately 45-50 mph in top gear). The speed range depends to some extent on the model. Although a special 'dephasing' vibration damper is fitted on each side of the engine, this arrangement does not entirely eliminate the vibration period.

Fortunately it is possible to 'drive through' the critical speed range and the engine should be capable of revving smoothly to over 6000 rpm.

Some engines develop slight piston slap — evidenced by a light tapping from the crankcase area — after moderate mileages have been covered but experience has shown that this does no harm and that the engine will continue to run for a long time in this condition.

Any engine which has covered a high mileage will, of course, have been subject to the usual wear-and-tear, so check for such obvious pointers as oil or water leaks, smoke from the exhaust and suspicious noises when the engine is revved up, when it is cold and also at running temperature. Carry out as extensive a test run as possible, so that any misfiring, knocking or lack of power can be detected.

Many servicing and repair jobs can be carried out without removing the engine from the car. These include top-overhauls, decarbonizing and attention to the valves and valve gear, fitting a new timing chain and sprockets and removing the engine sump, which allows the oil pump to be taken off and the connecting-rod bearings to be attended to.

When the degree of wear calls for a more thorough overhaul, such as attention to the pistons, the cylinder barrels, the crankshaft or the camshaft, the engine will have to come out. As we explain in Chapter 9, this should be well within the scope of a d.i.y. owner.

A good point is that a liner-piston kit consisting of matched sets of pistons, rings and cylinder barrels can be easily fitted instead of reboring the cylinders and fitting oversize pistons.

It is important to check the exhaust system for general corrosion and for rusting of the rear section from the inside, due to condensed water accumulating in it.

This is one of the few weak points on the Renault 12. Incidentally it's no use drilling a small hole in the lowest point in the silencer to allow the water to drain out. Many owners have tried this trick, but unfortunately it doesn't work!

Genuine Renault exhausts are not cheap, so if the exhaust is suspect — and remember that this can result in an MoT test failure — the best plan is to have a replacement fitted by one of the free-fit exhaust firms.

Performance tests

In Chapter 2 we give some typical performance figures for the various models. Of these, the acceleration times give the best indication of the overall efficiency of the car.

To avoid any risk of blowing-up the engine when checking the maximum speeds in the gears don't be tempted to use full throttle for longer than necessary and *never* over-rev the engine in neutral — especially if the car does not belong to you!

As far as fuel consumption is concerned, it is difficult to suggest an acceptable figure, since this will depend on road and traffic conditions, the load carried and, above all, on the way in which the car is driven. To be realistic, the figures quoted (like all the performance figures) should be regarded as only representative averages and should not be interpreted too strictly.

Transmission checks

If the clutch does not free cleanly or slips on taking-up the drive, one must first suspect that the cable is sticking or is incorrectly adjusted. Otherwise the trouble must lie in the clutch, and renewing this unit can be a fairly expensive job unless you are prepared to do the work yourself.

To change the clutch the gearbox must be removed, which in turn entails disconnecting the front-wheel drive shafts. This in itself should not pose any problems for a practical owner, but a snag which does sometimes crop up is that a drive shaft may stick on the splines at the inner end and when this happens special tools should be used to remove it. In such cases the work should be left to a Renault dealer.

This also applies, of course, if the same problem arises when it becomes necessary to change a worn drive shaft and universal joint assembly.

Incidentally, the wear on the joints depends to a great extent on the sort of use that the car has had. If the majority of the driving has been in towns with frequent acceleration and use of full steering lock, the joints will wear out much more quickly than if the car is driven mostly in the country or on relatively straight roads and motorways.

The joints cannot be purchased separately. They are supplied only as assemblies with the drive shafts, but less expensive alternatives to the Renault spares can be obtained from specialist firms.

On any high-mileage car it is not unusual for the synchromesh mechanism to be weak on second or third gear and a badly worn gearbox may also show signs of jumping out of these gears on the overrun. Obviously such a car should be avoided, or allowance should be made for the cost of fitting a reconditioned gearbox. Repairs are seldom economic.

If oil leaks from the point at which the drive shafts enter the gearbox or automatic transmission, renewal of the seals is normally a dealer job — so make a careful check for leakage here. It is reassuring to know, however, that this fault is fairly rare.

The automatic transmission offered as an alternative to the synchromesh gearbox has proved to be very reliable in service. Apparent faults can often be corrected by simple adjustments, but this work does call for specialized knowledge and equipment, especially where the electronic control unit is concerned. If you have any doubts about the transmission, it would obviously pay to consult a Renault dealer.

The suspension and steering

As we have indicated in Chapter 2, the steering should be light and positive, although the nose-heavy design of the car does create a good deal of understeer (a tendency to run wide) when cornering fast.

If the steering is stiff or, conversely, feels sloppy and imprecise, the trouble may lie in the rack-and-pinion unit, but is more likely to be caused by faulty steering linkage and front suspension parts.

Check the grease-seals on the front hub swivel ball joints, and the joints and the hub bearings themselves for wear as described in Chapter 14. If these check-out satisfactorily there is little that an owner can do except to have the front-wheel alignment and the steering geometry accurately measured. Preferably leave this to a Renault dealer, who will have the necessary equipment and will know where to look for any possible faults.

A full steering-geometry check should also be made if the treads of the front tyres show signs of uneven wear. It can be expensive to neglect this symptom.

The braking system

We have mentioned the hydraulic braking system in Chapter 2 and there is little that needs to be added here, except to say that Renault 12 brakes do not develop any troubles which are peculiar to these models alone.

If the brakes do not pull the car up smoothly and all-square when tested on a smooth, dry road, normal braking faults such as worn friction linings, leaking piston seals or seized pistons in the hydraulic cylinders or front-brake calipers, a weak vacuum servo, when fitted, or a faulty or incorrectly adjusted rear brake pressure limiting valve, are all possible points for investigation. This work is covered in Chapter 15.

4 Planned servicing
Preventive maintenance

In this and other chapters, we emphasize the importance of *preventive* maintenance — the avoidance of trouble before it becomes serious, or can result in a roadside breakdown.

The official Renault diagnostic-maintenance scheme calls for a visit to the lubrication bay once in every 3000 miles, or at least once in every six months, and a very thorough diagnostic check-up between 6000 and 9000 miles, or at least once a year.

The full diagnostic routine, however, would probably take the average owner, using only the limited facilities available in the home garage, the better part of a weekend to complete.

The home-servicing scheme outlined in the following pages has therefore been adapted from the official maintenance schedule so as to spread the work-load as much as possible. It also has the advantage of introducing more frequent checks on some items — particularly those associated with safety — than would be the case if a full diagnostic-maintenance check were to be deferred for the maximum recommended interval of one year or 9000 miles.

A question that often arises is whether one should service on a mileage or time basis.

If the car is used mostly for shopping and for an occasional week-end run into the country, of course, the mileage will not accumulate very quickly. While the car is standing idle the contact-breaker gap or the tappet clearances will not be increasing, the brake shoes or pads will not be wearing away and other parts will not require the checks and adjustments called for in the maintenance schedule.

In such cases servicing according to the mileage intervals quoted makes sense. There are cases, however, which justify — for some items — servicing on a time basis rather than by the mileage covered. For example, the engine oil will deteriorate much more quickly when short runs and frequent starts from cold cause excessive condensation of water and acids in the cylinders and sump and will require more frequent changing. The tyres will probably lose pressure whether the car is running or standing unused and the battery will be subject to slow self-discharge.

The brake fluid slowly absorbs moisture from the air, due to 'breathing' through the vent in the fluid-reservoir filler cap and through slightly porous hoses and the wheel cylinder seals. It will need to be changed after 12–24 months to avoid the risk of brake failure due to the fluid boiling in the wheel cylinders after a spell of hard braking.

The maintenance schedule must therefore be approached in a certain spirit of compromise, depending on the sort of use that the car receives.

Vital checks

A major drawback of do-it-yourself servicing in the home garage is the tendency of most owners to ignore the underside of the car: a case of out of sight, out of mind, perhaps?

Don't be tempted to crawl under the car when it is supported only by a jack or by a pile of bricks, however. A pair of drive-on wheel ramps will usually give enough clearance, or the car can be taken to your neighbourhood dealer at least twice a year to be put on a lift or over a pit so that the whole of the underside can be thoroughly inspected at leisure. It is well worthwhile to pay for this service, if necessary, or to hire a self-service bay if a garage is operating this scheme in your district.

If the underside is coated with mud and filth, it will obviously pay to hose it down thoroughly, or better still to have it steam-cleaned, before starting work. Garages which service commercial vehicles usually have steam-cleaning equipment, but the cost of the work, although well worthwhile, is not cheap.

Now for the vital check points:

First go over the whole of the underside of the car for any signs of flaking paint, peeling underbody coating, if this has been applied, and the beginning of rust. Pay particular attention to the sub-frame and the areas around the suspension mountings.

Check the brake pipes inch by inch for any signs of chafing, rust or pitting. A small corrosion pit can eat through a new pipe within two years, causing a pin-hole leak which may result in complete loss of brake fluid.

Check the flexible brake hoses for perishing, chafing and leakage from the unions.

There will probably have been some oil leakage from the engine and transmission units, but a heavy leak obviously calls for investigation.

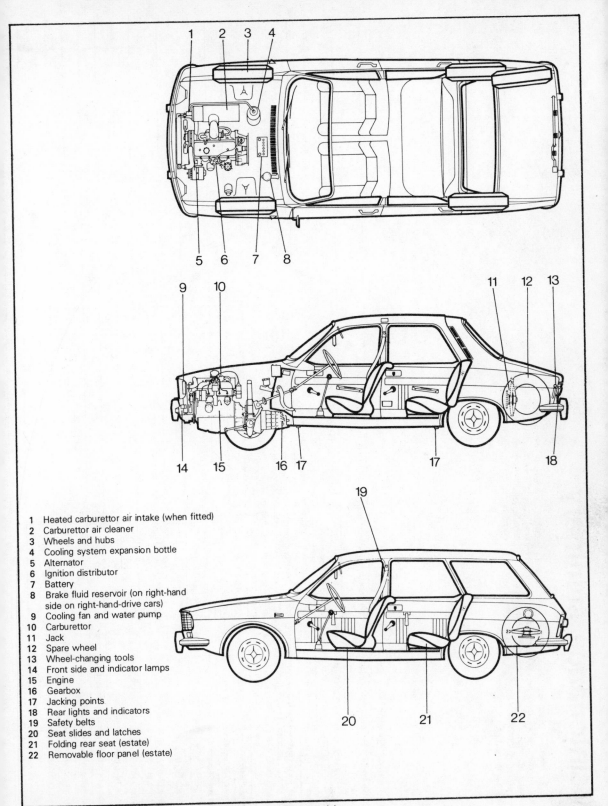

1 Heated carburettor air intake (when fitted)
2 Carburettor air cleaner
3 Wheels and hubs
4 Cooling system expansion bottle
5 Alternator
6 Ignition distributor
7 Battery
8 Brake fluid reservoir (on right-hand
   side on right-hand-drive cars)
9 Cooling fan and water pump
10 Carburettor
11 Jack
12 Spare wheel
13 Wheel-changing tools
14 Front side and indicator lamps
15 Engine
16 Gearbox
17 Jacking points
18 Rear lights and indicators
19 Safety belts
20 Seat slides and latches
21 Folding rear seat (estate)
22 Removable floor panel (estate)

Fig. 4.1 Some important maintenance points on the saloon and estate models.

Maintenance summary

This chart has been arranged to show at a glance the frequency with which the various jobs must be done. The items which make up a complete service can thus be identified and the work spread over several week-ends, if necessary. Remember that the columns are cumulative: the 3000 mile jobs must be repeated at 6000 and 9000 miles, the 6000 mile service at 12 000 miles (plus the jobs in the 12 000 mile column), and so on

	Weekly or before a long journey	Every 3000 miles (5000 km) or 3 months	Every 6000 miles (10 000 km) or 6 months	Every 12 000 miles (20 000 km) or 12 months	Every 27 000 miles (45 000 km) or 3 years
Vital safety checks					
Wheels and Tyres Check tyre pressures when cold. Watch for signs of uneven wear. Check tightness of wheel nuts	•				
Brake Fluid Reservoir Check level of fluid (this is a precautionary check only – topping-up should be required only at long intervals, unless a leak has developed in system)	•				
Brakes Check pedal travel; adjust brakes if necessary. Inspect brake pipes and hoses for leakage		•			
Brakes – Preventive Check Check thickness of linings. Check operating cylinders for leakage. Blow out dust. Check thickness of disc-brake friction pads. Check handbrake adjustment. Check pipes and flexible hoses for chafing. Renew all flexible hoses and rubber seals in braking system after 40 000 miles (65 000 km) or 3 years in service. Change fluid after 1–2 years in service			•		
Wheels Remove road wheels, wash and examine for possible damage			•		
Exhaust System Check for corrosion, leakage and security of attachments			•		
Lighting System Check headlamp beam alignment, lamp glasses for cracks, side, tail and indicator lamps for blackened bulbs, rusty contacts and water in lampholders		•			
Lubrication					
Engine Check oil-level and top-up if necessary (check daily if engine is worn and also when refilling with fuel on long run)	•				
Engine Drain oil and re-fill sump. Renew oil-filter element		•			
Ignition Distributor Lubricate					
Gearbox or Automatic Transmission Check oil level			•		
Synchromesh gearbox Drain oil and refill		•			
Automatic transmission Drain and refill every 18 000 miles					
Oil-can Lubrication Apply a few drops of oil to throttle linkage, handbrake linkage, door, boot and bonnet locks and hinges			•		
Speedometer Cable Lubricate inner cable with grease			•		

Servicing and adjustments

- **Cooling System** Check level in expansion tank and top-up if necessary
- **Cooling System** Check condition of hoses, and for leaks. Check tension of driving belt
- **Cooling System** Drain, flush and refill. Check operation of thermostat
- **Battery** Check level of liquid in cells
- **Windscreen Washer Reservoir** Check level of fluid. Add special anti-freeze solvent in winter
- **Engine** Check valve tappet clearances. Adjust if necessary
- **Engine** Service crankcase breather hoses
- **Engine** Clean the gauze flame-trap in breather pipe
- **Carburettor** Check slow-running adjustments
- **Carburettor Air-cleaner** Renew filter
- **Carburettor** Clean float chamber and jets
- **Fuel Pump** Check pump and clean filter if necessary
- **Sparking Plugs** Clean; Check gaps and re-set if necessary
- **Ignition System** Fit new sparking plugs and new contact-breaker points. Preferably do this at 10 000 miles (16 000 km)
- **Ignition Distributor** Clean or renew contact points and adjust gap. Clean distributor rotor and cap. Check timing. Preferably have system checked with electronic test-tune equipment
- **Clutch** Check cable adjustment
- **Automatic Transmission** Check and if necessary adjust kick-down switch and carburettor-to-governor cable
- **Drive shafts** Check for oil leakage and wear
- **Steering and Front Suspension** Check bellows on rack-and-pinion unit for splits or leakage. Check steering and suspension for damaged grease-retaining gaiters and wear
- **Steering and Front Suspension** Have front-wheel alignment and steering geometry checked with special equipment
- **Wheel Bearings** Check for leakage of grease, excessive end-play and noise when wheel is rotated
- **Wheels** Change from side to side at front and rear. Grease wheel studs. Have wheel balance checked
- **Braking System** Drain fluid from system, flush, refill and bleed-off air. This should be done every 1–2 years if mileage is less than 27 000 miles (45 000 km) in this period (see also **Vital safety checks** above)
- **Brake servo** Change air filter at 18 000 miles
- **Electrical System** Clean and tighten battery terminals. Check operation of charging system, starter motor, lights and instruments
- **Alternator** Have charging rate checked
- **Starter Motor** Check condition of brushes, commutator and pinion drive assembly every 36,000 miles
- **Road Test** Give car a thorough road test and carry out any adjustments required. If possible, have final check made with electronic test-tune equipment and check compression in cylinders. After test, check for oil, fuel, fluid or grease leaks at all plugs, flanges, joints and unions.

Examine the inner walls of the tyres for cuts or splits. It is surprising how often accidental damage occurs on the inside wall of a tyre, rather than on the outside, where it would be immediately visible. While checking the tyres, look for any signs of rubbing against the body when the springs are fully compressed or when the front wheels are turned to full lock.

Check the exhaust system for rust, damage and leakage and make sure that the supports are sound.

Finally, push, pull and shake all suspension and steering components vigorously, to show up any wear or loose attachments.

Your basic tool kit

The items listed below will be needed for routine servicing. More specialized tools can be added, as necessary, when repairs and overhauls are undertaken and a list of these is given at the beginning of each workshop manual section.

Special tools tend to be rather expensive, but you may be able to hire them from your local Renault dealer. The most frequently needed items, such as extractors, however, can normally be purchased from car accessory shops and these are usually cheaper than the 'official' service tools. Alternatively, there may be a shop in your neighbourhood which hires-out tools at reasonable charges.

A basic tool kit for routine servicing and minor repairs should include –

Set of open-ended or ring, or combination spanners, in metric sizes
Set of socket spanners with extensions and preferably a universal joint
Selection of screwdrivers, including two sizes for cross-head screws
Large and small adjustable spanners
Self-locking adjustable spanner (Mole wrench type)
Side-cutting and pointed-nose 6 in. pliers
Set of feeler gauges
Sparking plug gap-setting tool
Tyre-pressure gauge
Tyre tread-depth gauge
Engineer's hammer (ball pane)
Soft-faced hammer (with hide, plastic or copper faces)
Fine carborundum stone
Wire brush
Centre-punch, scriber and marking paint
Inspection lamp

A good tyre-pressure gauge is essential. Garage pressure gauges are not always as accurate as they should be: and pressures should always be checked with the tyres *cold*, which is obviously impossible if the car has to be driven to a garage or if pressures are checked during the course of a journey.

A tyre tread-depth gauge is an inexpensive item which will enable you to keep a check on the rate of wear of the tyres and will also indicate when they are due for replacement. The official regulation in Britain calls for 1 mm of tread over three-quarters of the width of the tread pattern, around the complete circumference of the tyre, but it is much safer to change the tyres when the treads are worn down to a depth of 2 mm.

A workbench will be needed for any jobs that are done on components that have been removed from the car, but it is quite possible to make do with a stout kitchen table, which can often be picked up inexpensively at an auction. If any but elementary servicing is carried out, a vice will be needed. This can often be obtained quite cheaply from a shop which deals in Ministry surplus equipment.

Turning the engine when making adjustments

When the crankshaft has a starting handle dog the easiest way to turn the engine is, of course, to use the handle.

In the case of a later car which does not have a starting handle, either engage top gear and push the car backwards and forwards, or jack-up one front wheel and turn the wheel with top gear engaged. *In both cases make sure that the ignition is switched off or the ignition distributor cap removed, to prevent the engine starting with the gear engaged.*

Some garage mechanics become adept at turning the engine by operating the starter motor for a few seconds at a time, but this method is only justifiable as a time-saver to obtain approximately the correct position of the flywheel. Final adjustment must be made by one of the methods just described, since accuracy is essential when setting the ignition timing, or adjusting the valve-clearances.

Working beneath the car

If an inspection pit is not available, a pair of drive-on wheel ramps will also be needed. A cheaper alternative is a pair of adjustable axle stands. These have the advantage of leaving the wheels free to rotate. On the other hand, it takes only a minute or two to drive the front or rear wheels on to a pair of ramps, whereas both sides of the car must be jacked-up to allow stands to be placed below the jacking points.

For obvious reasons, ramps or axle stands which lift only one end of the car must not be used when checking the oil-levels.

Finally, never be tempted to work beneath the car when it is supported only by the jack or by an insecure pile of bricks.

Part two

5 Trouble-shooting
Systematic diagnosis

The risk of an unexpected breakdown must obviously be greatly reduced by regular servicing. The work described in Chapter 4 can therefore be described as *preventive* maintenance in the best sense of the word; it aims at detecting or forestalling trouble before it becomes serious. Most faults, in fact, can be traced back to neglect at some stage. Dirt, lack of lubrication or incorrect adjustment are the most frequent culprits.

When devising the special trouble-shooting charts in this section, we had in mind mainly the practical owner, who often has to trace a fault without the benefit of a voltmeter, an ammeter, a vacuum gauge, a cylinder compression-pressure gauge or a simple stethoscope. These useful aids to diagnosis are usually conspicuous by their absence when the car breaks down miles from the home base!

The aim has been to produce a set of charts which will encourage a logical process of elimination. Inspired guesswork (intelligent intuition?) will sometimes get results, but systematic investigation will usually be less time-consuming in tracking-down obscure faults — although there are, of course, occasions on which the possibility of a particular fault can be assumed with a fair amount of certainty.

Take the case of a normally well-behaved engine that refuses to fire from cold after the car has been parked in the open during a spell of damp, misty weather, for example. Condensation on the high-tension leads, ignition coil, distributor, and sparking-plug insulators is almost a certainty, and a spray with one of the water-repelling aerosol fluids, or a wipe with a dry cloth, will usually be all that is needed to restore normal starting.

Similarly, if an engine runs well, but is a brute to start from cold, suspect too weak a starting mixture. Make sure that the mixture control is operating properly and that the petrol pump is delivering plenty of fuel. If the engine is reluctant to start when hot, on the other hand, check for an over-rich mixture. In either case, if the carburation seems to be satisfactory, the ignition system should be checked-over, following the step-by-step charts in this chapter.

Now a word as to how to use the trouble-tracing charts.

By reading vertically down the column, under the various symptoms, the most likely causes of the trouble can be picked out and eliminated one by one. Alternatively, by reading horizontally across the chart, a combination of different symptoms will often point pretty conclusively to one particular fault which is causing the trouble.

In some cases, these charts cover alternative types of equipment. To find out which items apply to your model, consult the Specifications and Overhaul Data at the end of this book.

Preventing trouble and restoring performance

There is a great deal to be said for carrying out a systematic inspection of the car at regular intervals — say, every 5000-6000 miles — in order to detect any incipient trouble and to correct any faults which may exist.

A ten-point check and tune-up to restore engine efficiency is outlined on page 19. A suggested routine for a more thorough check of the whole car is given in the fault-tracing and condition report sheet. If these checks are conscientiously carried out and any necessary adjustments are made, they will restore 'new car' performance on a vehicle that is in reasonably good mechanical condition. Any major faults which are present, such as loss of engine compression, and transmission or similar troubles, will, of course, require attention as soon as possible.

An inspection record of this type has, in itself, a number of advantages. Not only does it ensure that no item is overlooked, but it also enables the general condition of the car to be assessed at a glance. If completed systematically at each inspection period and filed for reference purposes, it will serve as a guide to the reconditioning required and as a check on the performance of each item.

When made out for the first time, as with a newly-purchased used car, the chart is almost certain to reveal defects that might otherwise have been unsuspected and that might have developed into major troubles.

Inspection record

Vehicle make and year_____
Capacity or horse power_____
Reg. number_____
Speedometer reading_____
Date of inspection_____

Engine and accessories

Compression

Tappets: clearance; noise

Valve gear: noise; cover gaskets

Timing gears or chain: noise; backlash

Cylinder head: nuts; gaskets

Manifolds: securing nuts; gaskets; air or gas leaks

Driving belts: fan; dynamo; accessories

Water pump: leakage; effectiveness

Radiator: water level; leakage; filler cap; condition of core; shutters; relief valve; overflow pipe

Oil leaks: crankcase; pipes and unions; timing covers; main bearings; drain plugs

Oil filters

Engine mountings

Carburettor and fuel pump

Jets

Float chamber level

Cold starting device: interconnecting linkage thermostat; dashboard control

Fuel pump: effectiveness; delivery pressure

Filters: carburettor; petrol pump; air cleaner

Ignition system

Contact breaker points: gap; condition

Rotor: condition

Distributor cap: cleanliness; cracks; tracking

Timing control: manual; centrifugal; suction operated

Coil and wiring: efficiency; condition of high and low tension wiring; support

Sparking plugs: gap at points; condition of points and insulators; washers

Electrical system

Dynamo or alternator: charging rate

Dynamo brushes and commutator: burning or pitting; chatter and sparking

Dynamo or alternator drive: condition of belt, tension

Voltage regulator

Ammeter: accuracy

Battery: acid level; specific gravity; voltage of each cell; connections; corrosion

Lights

Headlamps: focus and alignment; condition of reflectors

Side lamps

Tail lamps

Stop lamp

Other lamps: ignition warning; interior; trafficators

Switches and fuses

Electrical accessories

Windscreen wipers: efficiency; noise; condition of blades

Indicators

Starter: efficiency; condition of pinion and fly-wheel teeth

Horns

Interior heater

Defroster

Radio

Steering

Lost motion

Stiffness

Front axle alignment: toe-in; castor and camber angles

Swivels and bushes

Front hub bearings

Steering linkage and joints

Suspension

Springs: condition

Shock absorbers: effectiveness; fluid leaks; security of attachments

Torque reaction rods or cables: adjustment; security of attachment

Brakes

Pedal travel

Condition of rods or cables

Hydraulic system: fluid level; leakage from pipe lines, choked pipes, air in system

Handbrake: adjustment; condition of ratchet

Servo mechanism: vacuum servo; pipe lines

Bodywork

General appearance

Windows: winding controls; glass; channels

Doors: alignment; buffers; locks; check straps

Sunshine roof: operation; water leaks

Seats: condition of springs; adjustments

Bumpers: condition; attachments

Tool kit

Fire extinguisher, safety belts

Transmission

Clutch: adjustment

Backlash: in universal joints; in back axle; in gearbox

Rear axle: leakage

Wheels

Rims: buckling; rust

Wheel nuts: tightness; condition of studs; splines on knock-off wheels

Tyres

Pressures

Tread wear

Condition of sidewalls

Valves and caps

Road test

Engine	Clutch	Gearbox	Suspension	Back axle
Ease of starting	Slip	Noisy gears	Comfort	Noise on drive
Oil pressure when hot	Fierceness	Synchromesh operation	Roll on corners	Noise on overrun
Idling	Spinning	Preselector operation		Noise on corners
Acceleration	Unusual noises	Vibration on gear lever	**Brakes**	
Maximum speed		Gears jumping out of mesh	Power	**Steering**
Fuel consumption	**Propeller shaft**		Balance	Positiveness
Oil consumption	Vibration	**Instruments**	Smoothness	Castor action
Engine temperature	Noise	Functioning	Judder or squeal	Wander
Exhaust: noise, restriction; smoke		Accuracy	Binding	Road shocks at steering wheel
General noise, fumes				

Ten-point engine check and tune-up

The ten-point check on engine efficiency described in this section carries the principle of preventive maintenance, already outlined in Part 1, a stage further.

The object of an engine tune-up at an intermediate stage is to check deterioration: to restore the keen edge of engine efficiency, with a bonus in the form of improved performance and better fuel consumption. A good time to carry it out would be between the 5000-6000 miles services.

1 Electrical check

The effectiveness of the ignition system depends on sound electrical connections throughout the low-tension and high-tension wiring. Check them systematically, starting at the battery terminals and the earthing strap, and working via the ignition switch to the low-tension terminals on the ignition coil, and from there to the terminal on the side of the ignition distributor.

Check the security of the high-tension leads in the distributor cap and coil by lightly tugging them. Bear in mind that modern carbon-trace ignition cables usually have a. life of about two years. After that, misfiring is increasingly likely. A new set of leads will often rejuvenate an engine.

2 Check carburettor and manifold flange nuts

The nuts must not be loose but must never be overtightened — particularly the carburettor flange nuts — owing to the risk of distorting or cracking the flanges, a fault which is a common cause of air leakage into the induction system, resulting in a weak mixture, misfiring and difficult starting.

3 Clean the carburettor filter (when fitted) and the float chamber

Traces of sediment or water in the float chamber can upset the carburation and cause misfiring.

4 Fuel pump check

If the fuel pump does not deliver its maximum output when the engine is operating under full-throttle, continuous high-speed conditions, fuel starvation may cause severe exhaust-valve burning and possibly piston failure. If in doubt, have the pump checked by a garage, using a special flow-test rig.

5 Check the ignition distributor and contact-breaker

Peak efficiency cannot be expected if the contact-breaker points are dirty, badly pitted or incorrectly gapped. Distributor checks are covered in the section dealing with the ignition system.

6 Check the ignition timing

Again refer to the section dealing with the ignition system. The correct ignition timing is critical, affecting both performance and fuel consumption.

7 Remove and check the sparking plugs

The plugs are a good guide to running conditions, as shown by the colour illustrations in this chapter. Clean them if necessary and re-set the gaps. Carry out a compression check (below) before refitting them.

8 Compression test

The compression check gives a reliable indication of the efficiency of the valves, piston rings and cylinder bores. A compression gauge is not expensive. The simple type which combines a compression gauge with a tyre-pressure gauge will give reliable readings.

Bring the engine to normal running temperature. Remove all the sparking plugs and wedge or tie the throttle fully open. The compressions should be recorded at normal cranking speed which must remain constant throughout the test, so the battery must be well charged.

Make a note of the number of pulsations required to obtain a maximum gauge reading for the first cylinder tested. The same number of crankshaft revs should be used when testing the other cylinders.

When the first set of readings has been recorded, repeat the tests with approximately a tablespoonful of engine oil injected into each cylinder. Higher readings may now be obtained on some or all of the cylinders, indicating that the oil has sealed any leakage past the piston rings that was occurring during the first tests.

Any remaining differences between the maximum pressures recorded for the individual cylinder which exceed about 10lb per sq. in. are probably due to leakage past the valves (possibly due to wrong valve clearances). It is also possible that the cylinder head gasket is leaking, but this would normally cause overheating and, in some case, misfiring.

9 Check carburettor idling adjustments

Refit the plugs and adjust the carburettor idling speed and mixture strength. These adjustments are fully described in the chapter dealing with the carburettor and fuel system.

10 Road test

Carry out a thorough road test as described in the section which deals with vetting a used car. Record the figures and file them for reference when the next tune-up is carried out. 'Before and after' comparisons will then quickly show up any loss of efficiency and indicate the need for further action.

At-a-glance trouble-shooting chart 1
Engine faults - key chart

Symptoms

	Engine will not start	Starts but will not keep running	Stalls during normal running	Poor idling	Misfiring at all speeds	Not giving full power or revs	Fuel consumption excessive	Oil consumption excessive	Pinking or detonation	Over-heating, pre-ignition, running-on	Unusual noises
Carburation and Fuel System Chart 5	●	●	●	●	●	●	●		●	●	
Ignition System Chart 4	●	●	●	●	●	●	●		●	●	
Electrical System Chart 10	●										
Mechanical Faults Chart 2	●	●	●	●	●	●	●	●	●	●	●
Cooling System Chart 3						●	●	●	●	●	

First - Check your plugs

Normal
Nose lightly coated with grey brown deposits. Electrodes not burning unduly – gap increasing about .001 in. per 1000 miles. Plugs ideally suited to engine.

Carbon fouling
Deposits can short circuit the firing end. If recommended plug is fitted check for over-rich mixture, faulty choke mechanism or clogged air cleaner.

Oil fouling
Deposits can short circuit the firing end and this weakens or eliminates the spark. May be caused by worn valve guides, bores or piston rings or by running in an overhauled engine.

Overheating
Likely causes are overadvanced ignition timing, wrong grade of plug, use of too low octane fuel, weak mixture, or cooling system troubles.

At-a-glance trouble-shooting chart 8
Steering and controlability

Symptoms

Probable causes	Excessive free movement at steering wheel	Car wanders, or 'oversteers' excessively	Car pulls to one side	Heavy steering	Wheel wobble or vibration at steering wheel	Rattle or knock from beneath front floor near passenger's feet	Knock from base of steering column
Incorrect tyre pressures		•	•		•		
Rear tyre pressures too low		•					
Incorrect steering geometry and/or front-wheel alignment		•	•		•		
Tyres 'out of round,' or unbalanced tyres and wheels — have front and rear wheels balanced regularly					•		
Worn or incorrectly adjusted steering and suspension joints and/or wheel hub bearings	•	•	•		•		
Worn or incorrectly adjusted steering rack-and-pinion	•		•	•			
Distortion of column or rack-and-pinion unit caused by incorrect fitting				•			
Loose bolts holding rack-and-pinion unit to bulkhead	•				•	•	
Loose clamping bolt on steering column clamp or universal joint	•				•		•
Worn bush in rack-and-pinion unit						•	
Lack of oil in rack-and-pinion unit — check condition of telescopic gaiters				•		•	
Accidental damage — have suspension and steering units checked by authorized dealer			•	•			
Braking system faults — brakes unevenly adjusted, faulty hydraulic system, oil or grease on linings, brake discs running out-of-true. See Chart 9			•		•		
Suspension faults causing insufficient damping, sagging to one side or incorrect suspension height at front or rear — see Chart 7			•				

At-a-glance trouble-shooting chart 9
Braking system

This chart covers the most common faults in the full range of braking systems — all-drum, disc-and-drum and disc-and-drum and servo-assisted installations. When disc brakes or a servo are not fitted, the relevant items in the chart do not, of course, apply

Symptoms

Probable causes	Excessive pedal travel	Pedal feels spongy	Brakes lack power	Brakes bind or fail to release fully	Unbalanced braking — locking or pulling to one side	Brake judder	Brake squeal	Rapid wear of linings
Brakes incorrectly adjusted	•		•	•	•			•
Fluid level in reservoir too low		•	•					
Rubber seals in hydraulic cylinders swollen		•	•	•	•			•
Wheel cylinder or caliper piston seized			•		•			•
Leakage past seals in main or wheel cylinders, or from pipeline	•	•	•		•			
Internal fluid leak in servo (level in reservoir falls without visible external leak)		•						
Accumulation of brake dust in drums			•			•	•	
Badly-scored discs or drums			•		•			•
Worn wheel bearings	•		•			•	•	
Wrong type of friction linings fitted			•		•	•	•	•
Brakes 'fading' due to excessive use or wrong grade of linings	•		•					
Brake fluid boiling in wheel cylinders — pump all fluid out of system, refill with correct fluid and bleed brakes			•					
Master-cylinder, wheel cylinder or caliper bolts loose			•		•	•	•	
Air in system — requires bleeding		•	•					
New linings or pads not bedded-in		•	•					
Disc running out of true or drums distorted						•		
Water, oil or brake fluid on linings	•		•		•	•	•	
Servo defective			•	•				
Servo vacuum hose leaking or non-return valve faulty			•					
Pedal push-rod incorrectly adjusted				•				•
Handbrake operating levers or cable guides seized with rust or mud — brakes remain on or partly applied				•				•
Faulty rear-brake pressure-regulating valve					•			
Worn steering and suspension parts — see Charts 7 and 8					•			

At-a-glance trouble-shooting chart 5

Carburettor and fuel system

The faults in this chart are confined to the carburettor and fuel system. Some of the symptoms may be caused by other faults, which are dealt with in Charts 2, 3, 4.

Symptoms

Probable causes	Engine will not start	Starts but will not keep running	Stalls during normal running	Poor idling	Misfiring at all speeds	Not giving full power or revs	Fuel consumption excessive	Pinking or detonation	Overheating, pre-ignition, running-on
Carburettor(s)									
No petrol in float chamber — petrol tank empty, float needle valve sticking faulty fuel pump, filter clogged, petrol pipe obstructed, pipe union loose (see *Petrol Pump, Pipes and Tank*)	●	●							
Mixture (choke) control not lowering jet fully (S.U. carburettor)		●	●						
Hydraulic damper needs topping-up (S.U. carburettor)	●	●			●	●	●		
Carburettor suction piston sticking (S.U. carburettor). Choked jets (Zenith, Solex, Weber carburettors)	●	●	●		●	●	●		
Carburettor flooding — float needle valve not seating, fuel pump pressure too high	●	●	●	●	●	●	●	●	●
Air leakage past carburettor or manifold flanges	●	●	●	●	●	●	●		
Water or sediment in float chamber	●	●	●	●	●	●		●	●
Idling speed and mixture adjustments incorrect	●	●	●	●	●	●		●	●
Twin carburettors not properly synchronized				●	●	●	●		
Wrong jet needle, jet or piston spring fitted (S.U. and Stromberg carburettors). Wrong size of jet, faulty acceleration pump (Zenith, Solex, Weber carburettors)				●		●	●		●
Carburettor icing-up internally (normal running restored when carburettor warms-up). See also *Air Cleaner*				●	●	●	●	●	●
Petrol pump, pipes and tank									
Electric pump — dirty filter, poor electrical connections, dirty contacts		●	●						
Mechanical pump — dirty filter, air leak at filter cover flange	●	●	●	●	●	●		●	●
Electrical or mechanical pump — delivery pressure excessive	●	●	●	●	●	●		●	●
Fuel pipes — clogged, loose unions, vapour-lock in fuel pipe	●	●	●	●	●	●	●		
Petrol tank — empty (fuel gauge may be giving wrong reading)	●	●	●	●	●	●			
Petrol tank — air-vent obstructed, internal filter clogged	●	●	●		●	●			
Petrol tank — air-vent obstructed, internal filter clogged	●	●	●		●	●			
Air cleaner									
Filter clogged, overdue for renewal						●	●		
Air intake not correctly positioned for summer or winter use or thermostatically-controlled flap not functioning properly (may cause carburettor icing in winter — see *Carburettor icing-up*)	●	●				●	●		

At-a-glance trouble-shooting chart 4
Ignition system faults

The faults in this chart are confined to the ignition system. Some of the symptoms may be caused by carburation, mechanical or cooling system faults. These are dealt with in Charts 2, 3, 5.

Engine running symptoms

Probable causes	Engine will not start	Starts but will not keep running	Stalls during normal running	Poor idling	Mis-firing at all speeds	Mis-firing at high speed	Not giving full power or revs	Fuel consumption excessive	Pinking or detonation	Overheating, pre-ignition, running-on
Battery voltage too low – discharged or defective battery, resulting in heavy 'coil robbing' due to current drain by starter	●									
Cold-start coil circuit (when fitted) defective	●	●								
Low-tension circuit – faulty ignition switch, loose connections, faulty earthing strap (engine or battery to frame)	●	●	●	●	●	●	●	●		
Sparking plugs – wrong gap, dirty or worn-out	●	●	●	●	●	●	●	●	●	●
Sparking plugs – wrong type fitted	●	●	●	●	●	●	●	●	●	●
Contact-breaker points – dirty or pitted, wrong gap, incorrectly assembled, sticking open	●	●	●	●	●	●	●	●	●	●
Contact-breaker – weak contact spring	●	●	●	●	●	●	●			
Contact-breaker – broken spring	●									
High-tension circuit – current leakage across coil, distributor cap or rotor: insulation cracked, dirty or damp	●	●	●	●	●	●	●	●		
High-tension leads – poor contact at terminals, breaks in internal conductors, leads shorting to earth or to each other, faulty suppressors (when fitted)	●	●	●	●	●	●	●	●		
Sparking plug leads – connected in wrong sequence	●									
High-tension polarity incorrect – ignition to coil low tension connections reversed	●	●	●	●	●	●	●			
Distributor cap centre contact broken or sticking	●	●	●	●	●	●	●	●		
Coil or condenser – open-circuit, short-circuit, intermittent faults	●	●	●	●	●	●	●	●		
Static ignition timing – incorrect		●	●	●	●	●	●	●	●	●
Centrifugal timing mechanism – not functioning correctly				●	●	●	●	●	●	
Vacuum timing mechanism – not functioning correctly				●	●	●	●	●	●	
Distributor – shaft bearing worn				●	●	●	●	●	●	

At-a-glance trouble-shooting chart 7

Suspension

This is a general trouble-shooting chart, applicable to most suspension systems using leaf springs, coil springs, torsion bars and also hydro-pneumatic systems (eg British Leyland Hydrolastics, Hydragas and other pressurized systems using gas and hydraulic fluid)

Symptoms

Probable causes	'Bouncy' ride – insufficient damping	Car too low at front and/or rear	Car sags to one side	Groaning or grunting from suspension	Squeak from front or rear suspension	Knock from front suspension	Knock from rear suspension	Rumble or whine from front or rear suspension
Weak or broken springs. Incorrect pressure in hydro-pneumatic system or loss of fluid	●	●	●					
Weak springs allowing suspension to hit bump stops						●	●	
Noisy damper valves in hydro-pneumatic system				●				
Broken check strap							●	
Faulty shock absorbers or hydro-pneumatic unit	●							
Worn shock absorber bushes or loose mountings						●	●	
Squeak from rubber components – to cure, spray with silicone fluid or brush on brake fluid (*not* mineral oil)					●			
Worn bushes in radius arms or links							●	
Worn bushes in tie-bars, suspension arms or linkage					●	●		
Worn or incorrectly adjusted wheel bearings						●	●	
Worn, unlubricated or incorrectly adjusted wheel bearings								●

At-a-glance trouble-shooting chart 6
Clutch and transmission

This chart deals only with manual transmissions. Automatic transmission torque converters and gearboxes are complex units and special test equipment, which is held by authorized dealers, must be used to diagnose faults in them

Probable causes	Clutch slip	Clutch judder or snatch	Rattle, knock or squeal from clutch	Difficulty in engaging gear	Jumping out of gear	Noisy gearbox	Rattle or buzz from gear lever	Rattle from transmission when idling	Knocking or clicking from front of car when cornering
Air in clutch hydraulic operating system – needs bleeding (hydraulically-operated clutches)				●					
Clutch adjustment incorrect	●			●					
Clutch driven plate – worn, or oil on friction lining	●								
Clutch release bearing dry and due for renewal			●						
Clutch driven plate buckled during assembly									
Clutch release mechanism worn		●	●	●					
Clutch hub splines worn		●	●						
Gears and/or bearings worn					●	●		●	
Gear teeth chipped						●			
Selector linkage worn or damaged				●	●		●		
Gear lever pivot and linkage worn or needs lubrication							●		
Synchromesh mechanism worn				●	●				
Noise caused by transfer-gears on some front-wheel drive models – difficult to cure at idling speed, but careful carburettor adjustment helps								●	
Universal joints at outer ends of driving shafts worn and due for renewal (front-wheel drive cars only)									●

At-a-glance trouble-shooting chart 3

Cooling system

This is a general chart covering water-cooled and air-cooled engines. All the items apply to water-cooled systems but only those marked with an asterisk affect air-cooled engines

Symptoms

Probable causes	* Overheating at normal atmospheric temperatures	* Overheating in very cold weather	* Engine slow to warm-up	* Engine does not reach normal running temperature	* Radiator needs frequent topping-up
* Fan belt – not correctly tensioned or broken	●				
Radiator filler cap – not sealing properly, or wrong pressure rating	●				●
Thermostat – faulty or wrong rating	●		●	●	
* Radiator or cooling fins – water or air passages clogged	●				
Water passages in cylinder head or block – choked by deposits of lime, rust or sludge	●				
Radiator – frozen at base (no anti-freeze, or too low a concentration)		●			
Water pump – inefficient or inoperative	●				
Air-lock – in cooling system or heater	●				
Water hoses – leaking (check with engine revved-up)	●				●
Water hoses – perished, collapsed or obstructed by disintegrated linings	●				●
Internal water or gas leakage – caused by faulty cylinder-head gasket, cracked head or cylinder block	●				●
Local boiling in cylinder head – rust and lime deposits, filler cap pressure rating too low, or cap leaking	●				●
* Ignition faults – retarded timing, pre-ignition or detonation (see Chart 4)	●				
* Carburation – faults causing weak mixture (see Chart 5)	●				
Brakes – binding (see Chart 9)	●				
* Exhaust system – choked or damaged, restricting flow of gas	●				
* Engine – assembled too tightly after overhaul	●				

At-a-glance trouble-shooting chart 2
Engine: mechanical faults and noise

Running conditions and probable causes	Tapping or clicking	Knock, tapping or light clatter	Clatter or knocking	Light clatter or chattering	High-pitched metallic tapping	Scraping noise	Knocking, rumbling or thumping	Lashing, rattling or grinding noise	Squeaks or whistles
Apparent source	Cylinder head or block	Cylinder head or top of block	Crankcase or front of engine	Cylinder head	Audible when accelerating	Cylinder block	Crankcase	Timing chain cover	Front of engine or near manifolds
Engine cold—worn pistons, rings, cylinder bores (piston slap)[1]		●							
Engine hot—worn little-end bearings[1]		●							
Engine hot, more evident when idling—worn camshaft bearings	●								
Valve-rocker clearances too great, worn valve-operating mechanism, bent push-rod	●			●					
Broken piston rings[2]						●			
Engine under load or when revved in neutral—big-end bearing wear[3]			●						
Engine under load and hot—'pinking' caused by pre-ignition or detonation[4]					●				
Crankcase, engine under load—main-bearing and/or crankshaft journal wear[3]							●		
Loose flywheel			●						
Occurring at high revs—valve-bounce (possibly weak valve springs)				●					
Loose or broken engine mounting			●						
Worn timing chain (when fitted). Defective chain tensioner								●	
Front of engine—loose crankshaft pulley or worn pulley key (can be mistaken for big-end bearing wear)							●		
Front of engine—worn, glazed or slipping fan belt. Worn or dry generator or fan-bearings. Noisy water pump bearing or seal									●
Vicinity of inlet and exhaust manifolds—loose manifold bolts or nuts, or defective gaskets									●

1 Noise can be reduced or eliminated by [...]

2 Badly-worn rings and grooves in pistons may [...]

3 Usually accompanied by low oil pressure

4 Check that correct grade of fuel is in use. Also see Chart 1

Dealing with dents, scratches and rust

One of the recurring themes in this book is 'Prevention is better than cure'. In Chapter 3 we emphasize the importance of making a careful check for rust. Here we are concerned with minimizing its effects. Neglect even a minor blemish, and you will find that rust can spread with alarming rapidity under the surrounding paintwork.

Dealing with scratches and chips

As shown in the first photograph, it is best to use a fine brush for touching-in small blemishes. If an aerosol paint spray is used it is difficult to confine the spray to a very small area. We give some notes on spraying larger areas at the end of this section.

Scrape any loose paint and rust from the area with the tip of a penknife blade, apply a rust-preventive, such as Zinc Plate, to the bright metal and then knife-on a thin layer of cellulose stopping, building up the level to slightly above the surrounding paintwork.

When the stopping is dry, rub it down with very fine wet-or-dry paper, used wet; with a smear of soap to prevent clogging. Then touch-in the area with the correct colour to match the surrounding finish.

Alternatively, your accessory shop may sell a card of special paint transfers which, when applied on a clean surface and rubbed down, produce an almost undetectable repair to a scratch or chip.

Removing dents

The second picture shows the sort of dent that can be dealt with at home by filling it with glass-fibre resin paste.

Rub down to bare metal, extending to about 2 in. beyond the edge of the dent, using 80 grit paper. Score the base and sides of the dent with a file or screwdriver to provide a key for the body filler, and apply this with a plastic spatula as illustrated until the level is above the surrounding metal.

If the dent is localized, it is usually a mistake to attempt to tap it out. The metal has probably been stretched, and too enthusiastic attempts at amateur panel-beating will turn the dent into a bulge—which must then be tapped back again so that the hollow can be built-up with body filler!

In the case of a large, shallow dent, however, the metal may simply have bulged inwards and can be

At-a-glance trouble-shooting chart 10

Electrical equipment

It has been possible to deal only with the broader aspects of electrical fault-tracing in this chart. Detailed diagnosis calls for the use of accurate instruments and a good deal of electrical know-how. It is best left to a qualified auto-electrician

Symptoms

Probable causes	Battery and Charging system				Starter motor		Lamps			
	Battery cells need frequent topping-up with water	Battery apparently not receiving sufficient charge	Battery will not hold charge	Starter does not turn engine, or rotates it slowly	Starter runs but pinion does not engage with flywheel gear	Starter pinion jams in mesh of flywheel gear	Headlamps give poor illumination when correctly aligned	Brightness of lights varies noticeably with engine speed	Lights flicker	Bulbs or light units burn out frequently
Battery discharged				●			●	●		
Battery electrolyte level too low or of wrong specific gravity		●	●							
Defective battery – sulphated or buckled plates		●	●	●			●	●		
Generator driving belt slipping		●						●		
Faulty generator		●						●		
Charging regulator defective or incorrectly adjusted. Charging rate too high or too low	●	●						●		●
Loose or high-resistance connections in charging circuit								●		
Loose or high-resistance connections in lighting circuits									●	
Corroded or loose battery terminals				●			●		●	●
Poor earth-return connections							●		●	
Leakage of current in car wiring			●							
Faulty starter switch				●						
Poor connections in starter circuit				●	●					
Dirty or faulty starter pinion drive					●	●				
Worn starter pinion teeth on flywheel ring gear						●				
Faulty starter motor				●						

persuaded to spring out again by applying pressure to the inside of the panel. When the inner side cannot be reached—for example in a double-skinned section of the body—the simplest plan is to drill a hole at the centre of the dent, insert a self-tapping screw and pull the dent out by gripping the head of the screw with a pair of pliers, a self-locking wrench, or a claw hammer. The hole can then be filled with stopper, sanded down and touched-in. Another ploy that has proved successful is to ease a deflated football bladder between the two skins of the bodywork, pump it up and pop the dent out.

3 Rubbing down the filler

Here the filler is being rubbed down with progressively finer paper, after the paste has hardened, until a good finish is obtained, to prepare the surface for spraying as described in Sections 8 and 9.

4 Dealing with badly-rusted panels

The corroded metal must be ruthlessly cut away until sound, bright metal is reached. When rust has attacked the back of a panel this may mean that an innocuous-looking dimpled area is converted into a fairly large hole with ragged edges, as shown in the photograph. These must be tapped back with a hammer to about ¼ in. below the level of the surrounding paintwork.

5 Glass-fibre repairs

A typical glass-fibre kit is shown in this photograph. It contains a supply of glass-fibre mat, which is used to cover the damaged area, tissue and ribbon to repair smaller areas, resin, hardener and filler powder, and often a stippling brush, a stirring rod and a mixing bowl. If the damaged area is a load-bearing one, the only safe repair is to have a patch welded in by a garage. You can then save money by filling and spraying the repaired area at home. If the part is unstressed, however, the sound edges should be tapped in until they are about ¼ in. below the surface of the surrounding metal and a glass-fibre patch can be applied.

6 Applying the glass-fibre mat

Here we show a piece of glass-fibre mat being applied to the damaged area. It is essential to follow the instructions which are supplied with each kit. The principle is to cut a suitably sized piece of mat, mix some resin and catalyst in the correct proportions, stipple the resin generously over the damaged area, apply the glass mat, thoroughly soak this with resin, and repeat the operation with a second layer of mat. If the damage is fairly extensive, a sheet of perforated zinc can be used to reinforce the glass-fibre. When repairing a rusty hollow section, a self-foaming plastic can be poured into the cavity until it overflows from the hole, quickly setting into a sufficiently rigid mass to provide a good support for the glass-fibre mat.

7 Preparing for spraying

When the resin has hardened, build up the external surface with the filler paste as shown in the picture. Use coarse emery paper, an emery disc in an electric drill, or a Surform file to obtain the correct profile. Then rub down the surface with 180 grade wet-or-dry emery paper, used wet, to blend the repair into the surrounding paintwork, followed by light rubbing with 400 grade, again used wet, and preferably with a trace of soap, until a silky smooth surface can be felt.

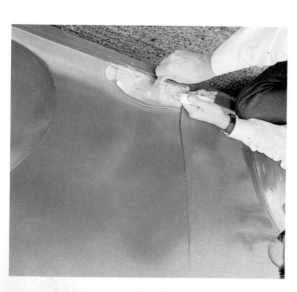

8 Masking-off and spraying

Special masking tape can be obtained from garages and accessory shops. Never use ordinary cellulose tape, which will lift during spraying. Tape around the area to be sprayed, and attach sheets of newspaper to this tape with a second strip of tape.

Allow sufficient space to blend-in the new paint gradually. If you spray right up to the masking tape, the paint will build up along the edge of the tape and leave a ridge when it is removed.

Aerosol paint spray cans are ideal for small jobs, but first practise spraying on a sheet of metal or hardboard. Spray guns are more expensive and call for experience to obtain really good results.

Wash the prepared surface and allow it to dry before applying at least two coats of primer. Keep the spraying nozzle about 6-9 in. away from the surface, as shown in the photograph. Rub down each coat with 400 grade paper. The first colour coat can then be sprayed on, again followed by a light rub down, before the next coat is applied. Apply further light coats until a good finish is obtained.

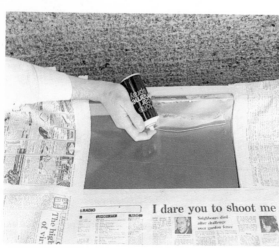

Blend the spray into the surrounding paintwork. The colour of the new paint will usually change slightly as it dries and the true colour may not be obtained until a day or so has elapsed.

9 Blending and polishing

After the new paint has hardened thoroughly — allow at least a week for this — the surface can be polished and blended in with the old paintwork by using a mild abrasive compound. Liquid metal polish, or one of the cleaners' sold by the car polish firms for removing the stale outer film from the paintwork (such as Colour Cut) will produce a good finish.

7 The Ministry Test
Will your car pass or fail?

When you submit your car for the MoT test, the chances are about one in three that it will fail at the first attempt.

This is, of course, an average failure rate for all the cars tested in Great Britain. A more encouraging aspect is that an experienced tester will tell you that in many cases these failures need never have occurred. The faults could have been detected by a practical owner and should have been put right before the car was taken to the testing station.

The value of the test is that it is essentially a safety check. Think of it, if you like, as an expert second opinion on the efficiency of your servicing during the past twelve months, covering such vital points as the brakes, steering, tyres, seat belts and the lighting system. Approach it in this spirit and you will give your car the best chance of passing with flying colours.

In the space available here it is not possible to give a detailed, point-by-point summary of the requirements laid down in the comprehensive Ministry tester's manual (which is revised from time to time to include additional items) but it *is* possible to provide an overall picture of the sort of checks that you can carry out at home.

A surprisingly large number of cars do not get even as far as a detailed inspection. The tester may fail your car if he finds any of the following faults –

Failure of the horn, windscreen wipers and washers to work; stop-lamps which have broken or dirty lenses or faulty bulbs (when two lamps are fitted they must light up simultaneously); direction indicators which do not flash at the correct rate of 60-120 flashes per minute, or have a faulty indicator light; a rusty or perforated exhaust pipe or silencer; shock absorbers which are so worn as to affect the controllability of the car; and bodywork faults such as loose or broken seat mountings, a faulty door lock or bonnet catch, or damaged or torn sections which might injure other road users.

Before going further, you might ask yourself, 'if this were a car belonging to a stranger, would I be completely happy to drive it?'

It is also reasonable to expect a refusal if the underside of the car is so caked with mud and grime that the tester cannot easily examine it, or if you cannot produce a previous test certificate or the vehicle registration book as evidence of the age of the car.

If you have carried out the checks described in Chapter 3, however, have, preferably, filled in a condition report sheet on the lines suggested in Chapter 5, and have conscientiously carried out the regular servicing outlined in Chapter 4, you should be able to face the test with confidence and we can now turn to some of the detailed checks which can be carried out at home. These form, in effect, a 'dummy run' for the actual test itself.

Checking the braking system

Begin by checking the 'feel' of the brake pedal, with the engine running if a servo is fitted. A 'spongy' pedal, or the need to pump it to take up excessive travel, will call for immediate investigation. Refer to Chart No. 9 to diagnose the most likely causes and turn to Chapter 15 for advice on how to put them right.

Next get under the car, and with an inspection lamp go over the flexible hoses, every inch of the rigid pipelines and the unions. Look for cracks in the hoses, corrosion of the pipelines and seepage of fluid from the unions. Make sure that there is no risk of the hoses being rubbed by the front wheels on full lock and that none of the rigid pipes is in danger of being chafed where it passes close to the underframe or through an opening. Pay particular attention to the handbrake operating cables and rods, looking for frayed cables, worn pivots and clevis pins, and any signs of binding in the mechanism.

Seepage of brake fluid or grease from the wheel bearings on to the brake drums, backplates, discs and calipers will immediately be obvious and would be an equally immediate cause for failing the car.

Check the handbrake for excessive travel and make sure that the ratchet holds securely.

The tester will pay particular attention to all these points before carrying out a brake test. You will not be able to measure the efficiency of the brakes – the minimum is 50% for the foot brake and 25% for the handbrake – but by testing the brakes at about 30 mph on a smooth-surfaced, traffic-free road you should be able to detect any lack of efficiency or a tendency to pull to one side or the other, or to lock one wheel prematurely.

A final point: before handing the car over to the tester, make sure that the brake fluid reservoir has been topped-up to the correct level.

Steering checks

It is reasonable to suppose that you would not allow your car to go for test if there was an obvious fault such as excessive lost motion at the steering wheel, tight steering, poor self-centring, a tendency to pull to one side or wheel-wobble. Apart from steering faults, one cannot rule out poor roadholding due to weak dampers or a generally tired suspension system.

Check through the symptoms listed in Chart No. 8 and then turn to Chapters 14 and 15 for the corrective action.

The Ministry inspection is not confined to the road test. The tester will raise the car on a lift, or place it over a pit and with the front wheels supported clear of the ground, will push, pull and tug at all the steering connections in order to detect worn joints or loose mountings.

You can forestall him by jacking up each wheel in turn, grasping it at top and bottom and rocking it to show up excess play in the wheel bearings and in the hub-carrier swivel joints. There should be just perceptible end-play in the wheel bearings. Any excessive movement calls for investigation. Next spin the wheel and listen for grinding or rubbing noises which would indicate the bearings are badly worn or are breaking up.

With both wheels lowered to the ground, get under the car and ask a friend to tug the steering wheel towards each lock in turn and release it, while you closely watch the steering joints for any signs of wear.

Nowadays, the joints are of the self-adjusting type, except where rubber bushes are used. It used to be said that if any slackness could be felt when the upper part of the joint was levered away from the lower part, replacement was indicated. Many modern joints, however, have a small amount of 'lift' when new, in order to increase their service life. With this type of joint, if the lower half can be raised by more than about 0.01 in. by exerting pressure with a lever pivoted against the inside of the wheel rim, renewal is probably necessary.

You may find that an eccentric type joint is fitted, however, which must be checked for wear by levering it *sideways* in relation to the ball-pin.

Obviously, accurate assessment of the amount of wear which is present calls for experience and that is why we recommend that the best check is to watch the joints while the steering wheel is tugged towards each lock and released. Sloppy joints will immediately show up under this treatment.

If the protective rubber boot on a joint is found to be damaged or displaced, the joint should be renewed as a safety precaution. The tester will probably condemn it, anyway.

The tyres

It should be obvious that tyres which are worn below the legal minimum of 1 mm of tread depth across at least three-quarters of the width of the tread, and around the whole of the circumference of the tyre, are potentially lethal and should not be found on a well-maintained car.

Not so obvious, however, are cuts or bulges on the inner walls of the tyres, or a damaged wheel rim which could cut the tyre or cause sudden loss of pressure. The tester will also look for uneven tread wear, which suggests steering or braking defects, and will immediately fail the car if he discovers an illegal mixture of cross-ply and radial-ply covers. If the tyres are of different types, the radials must always be fitted to the rear wheels. Obviously, it is best to avoid any mixture and stick to cross-plies or radials throughout.

Remember to check the spare wheel. The tester must assume that if you carry a spare you intend to use it if a puncture occurs, and it is therefore logical to fail the car if the spare wheel is fitted with a badly-worn or otherwise defective tyre, or one of the wrong type.

Bodywork condition

The tester will pay particular attention to the uderside of the vehicle. Vital components in this respect are the underframes, stressed body sills, suspension mountings and the floor pans, especially where the seat mountings and seat belt attachments are bolted through.

Never be tempted to try to camouflage badly-rusted, stressed areas by glass-fibre repairs. An experienced tester will spot this immediately and will refuse to pass the car until a proper repair has been made by welding-in new sections.

The lighting system

The requirements laid down in the tester's manual can be summed-up in a few words: all the lights on the car which are required by the Construction and Use Regulations must be working properly and the headlamps must be correctly aligned so that they do not dazzle other drivers when dipped.

So far as the standard lighting system is concerned, therefore, all that you have to do is check for a 'blown' bulb, a wiring fault, a poor earth contact or a faulty switch which prevents a light functioning, a cracked or missing lamp glass or a badly-rusted reflector.

It is not really practical to attempt to adjust the headlamp beams by aiming them at marks on a wall. There are too many sources of error and a proper check can be carried out so much more accurately by a garage, using an optical beam setter. If you have any doubts, have this check made before submitting the car for the test.

The seat belts

Finally, don't forget to check the seat belts and their mountings. The tester is justified in failing a car if he finds a loose or insecure mounting or a badly-frayed belt.

Part three

8 Strip, repair or replace?
Practical notes on overhauls

'Whip it off and fit a new one!' says the garage mechanic or knowledgeable friend dogmatically when a fault develops in a component which calls for more than a minor repair – and with high labour charges in mind you may feel inclined to agree with him.

But is he giving you good advice? Does it always make economic sense, for example, to fit a service-exchange starter motor? The answer is probably 'No,' if all that is required is a set of new brushes and cleaning up the commutator – but the works-reconditioned component has been fully overhauled and *does* carry a guarantee!

In the case of an alternator, on the other hand, it is almost certainly best to fit an exchange unit. It is possible to change the alternator brushes, but testing the diodes and the charging regulator should be left to a qualified auto-electrician.

Where safety is involved we think it better to renew all doubtful items. The hydraulic components in the braking system should be replaced as complete assemblies, for example, instead of trying to salvage them by fitting new rubber parts from an overhaul kit. New rubbers in scored or corroded bores can have very short lives! The same principle applies to steering gear parts.

Again, where the clutch is concerned, renew everything that can wear – in this case as a matter of sound economics. It is much too time-consuming to remove and strip the clutch later should a worn part fail.

Similarly, when you strip a worn gearbox you will probably end up by replacing most of the parts, so there may not be much difference between the cost of these and the price of a reconditioned exchange unit.

In subsequent chapters, and in the notes on engine overhaul which follow, we deal with this subject more fully, indicating those jobs which are likely to be beyond the skill or resources of the beginner, and suggesting 'repair by replacement' where this is likely to be more economical or more satisfactory.

A final point to bear in mind is that if special service tools will be needed to carry out an overhaul properly, the expense of these – assuming that they cannot be borrowed or hired – will seldom be justified for a one-off job.

Practical aspects of engine overhauls

It is possible to tackle virtually any degree of engine wear in the home garage by dividing the work into three stages and taking advantage of the replacement or reconditioned parts or assemblies which are available from specialist firms. The practical aspects of the work are fully covered in Chapter 9, so we can confine ourselves here to a brief discussion of the pros and cons of the various stages of overhaul, which can be summarized as follows –

Stage 1 Fitting new piston rings, including special oil-control rings, to the existing pistons.

Stage 2 Partial overhaul, including new special pistons with rings and gudgeon pins, fitting new connecting-rod bearings, exhaust valves, valve springs and timing chain.

Stage 3 Full overhaul, including fitting a new set of cylinder barrels, complete with a matched set of piston rings and gudgeon pins, together with a reground crankshaft, new bearing shells, a new flywheel, and a new camshaft, camshaft bearings, followers, timing chain and tensioner, plus any other auxiliaries which need to be replaced. Alternatively, a 'half-engine', 'short motor' or 'pin up' (these terms will be described later) or a reconditioned, exchange engine.

Even if you are a novice, you should be able to tackle Stages 1 and 2 with every prospect of success. If you have had some experience of working on engines, there is no reason why you should not carry out the more ambitious Stage 3 overhaul, provided that you are able to borrow or hire lifting tackle to remove and refit the engine (don't rely on the roof beam of a prefabricated garage to carry the weight of the engine) and can call on the assistance of a friend when an extra pair of hands is needed.

Bearing in mind these points, a brief run through the pros and cons of the different reconditioning methods may help you to come to the right decision.

Fitting new piston rings (Stage 1)

A set of special piston rings can deal successfully with bore wear up to a maximum of about 0.003–0.004 in. for each inch of cylinder diameter, but their effectiveness depends on correct fitting.

It is usually necessary to send the pistons to the firm

that supplies the rings so that the worn grooves can be machined to match the new rings. Since the connecting-rod eyes must be heated and special tools used when removing and refitting the gudgeon pins, it would probably be better to negotiate the whole deal with your Renault dealer.

Never be tempted to fit a set of oil-control rings to worn pistons without enlisting the help of a specialist supplier. At best the result may be disappointing; at worst, ring breakage may occur, scoring the cylinder walls and rendering a set of new barrels essential.

Oil consumption should remain within reasonable limits for about 10 000 miles after a Stage 1 overhaul. If it is proposed to sell or exchange the car within this mileage, therefore, the fitting of special rings alone may well be an economic proposition.

Stage 2 overhaul

If you intend to keep the car for a longer period, however, and it has not covered more than about 40 000 – 60 000 miles, serious consideration should be given to a Stage 2 overhaul.

Most of the work entailed will be the same as that required when fitting new rings alone but the replacement of the pistons and the connecting-rod bearings, combined with a top-overhaul and the fitting of new exhaust valves, and a set of valve springs, will give the engine a new lease of life.

'Intermediate engine overhaul' kits are available from specialist firms such as AE Edmunds Walker and can be ordered through your garage. They contain everything that is needed for a Stage 2 overhaul – pistons and rings, bearing shells, exhaust valves, valve springs, gaskets, jointing compound and even an oil filter and a piston-ring clamp.

Renault recommend, however, that if the cylinder bore ovality or taper wear exceeds about 0.006 in. (0.15 mm) a new set of cylinder barrels and pistons should be fitted. In practice, however, cylinder wear is often negligible even after high mileages. It is the rings which wear and cause loss of compression and high oil consumption.

Stage 3 overhaul

The simplest solution is to lift the engine out and install a reconditioned unit; or you can go to the other extreme and strip it right down, fit new or reconditioned parts as necessary and rebuild it.

If you decide to fit a 'recon' engine, you again have the choice of ordering a factory-rebuilt unit from your local dealer, or shopping around for a rebuilt engine at a lower price, among the smaller engineering firms which specialize in this work. The advertisements in the practical motoring papers will provide a list of prospects.

Owing to the specialized construction of these engines and the use of aluminium-alloy components, it would be wise to deal only with a reputable firm – say, one which is a member of the Federation of Engine Remanufacturers.

Reputable engine rebuilding firms usually offer a worthwhile guarantee, however. In such cases their units should be just as satisfactory as factory-rebuilt units.

Although these are known in the trade as 'full' engines, they are not in fact complete. You will have to remove the carburettor, manifolds, ignition distributor, starter, fuel pump, dipstick from your engine and fit them to the new unit – after suitably reconditioning them, of course.

It will probably be necessary also to remove and keep the securing studs, bolts and nuts for these items, which will not be supplied with the new unit. In some cases you may have to fit your own flywheel and valve cover, so check carefully just what is offered.

A cheaper proposition is the 'half engine' or 'short motor'. This consists of a cylinder block with new barrels and pistons, fitted with a reground crankshaft in new main bearings complete with reconditioned connecting rods, a reground camshaft, new or refaced cam followers and new timing sprockets. To this you add your own reconditioned cylinder head, the auxiliaries already mentioned and the other bits and pieces that go to make up a complete engine.

A short engine obviously entails a good deal more work on your part, but with a corresponding saving in expense. Few, if any, special tools are required and all the skilled work has been done for you.

Finally, the cheapest proposition is that known in the trade as a 'pin-up' – which sounds interesting, but in fact means simply that the parts supplied are limited to a reconditioned crankcase, cylinder barrels, pistons, crankshaft and connecting rods, ready-assembled for you to build into a complete engine, using your own new and reconditioned parts for the remaining items.

The time factor

If this is to be your first attempt at carrying out, say a partial engine overhaul, make sure that you allow plenty of time, plus a safety margin for unexpected delays. If you begin work on a Thursday evening, it should be possible to complete the preliminary dismantling on the cylinder head that night, so that any replacements that are found to be necessary and are not included in the intermediate engine overhaul kit referred to earlier can be obtained on Friday morning.

By making an early start on Friday it should be possible to lift the engine out, withdraw the connecting rods and pistons, have the old pistons removed and the replacements fitted by your Renault dealer, if necessary, reassemble the pistons and connecting rods (fitted with new bearing shells) and the cylinder barrels and finally turn your attention to decarbonizing the cylinder head and grinding-in the valves.

The whole of Saturday will probably be occupied in finishing off the bottom half of the engine, fitting a new filter, refitting the cylinder head, manifolds and carburettor, reinstalling the engine and making adjustments followed by a short test run.

9 The engine

In Chapter 8 we have explained how a do-it-yourself enthusiast can successfully tackle quite an ambitious engine overhaul without the need for special skills or an impressive array of workshop equipment.

The secret, of course, is to confine oneself, as far as possible, to straightforward stripping and assembly, leaving the trickier jobs to the experts.

The engine repairs and adjustments that can be tackled without the use of special tools and equipment are mainly influenced by the design of the cylinder head and valve-operating gear and, in the case of major overhauls, by the pistons, cylinder barrels, crankshaft and the crankcase components. Notes on the practical aspects of these components are given in the sections which deal with the individual units.

Briefly, the jobs that can be undertaken by a practical owner without removing the engine from the car (in addition to the usual maintenance tasks) are: valve clearance checks and adjustments; removing the cylinder head for decarbonizing and a top-overhaul; attention to the timing chain, tensioner and sprockets; changing the pistons and cylinder barrels; checking the oil pump, suction filter and pressure-release valve; and renewing the connecting rod big-end bearings – but not the main bearings, one of which cannot be removed with the engine *in situ.*

For other jobs the engine must be lifted out, either separately or complete with the gearbox or automatic transmission. Engine removal and refitting is discussed as a separate subject at the end of this chapter.

The type numbers of the engines used in the various UK models are shown on the next page and we have used these to identify the different units.

810-02 – 1289 cc engine fitted to L and TL models. This engine has a standard compression ratio of 8.5:1 for earlier models and 9.5:1 for TL models from October 1975 onwards. The engine is fitted with a single-choke Solex 32 EISA carburettor

810-05 – 1289 cc engine fitted to TS models. This unit has a compression ratio of 9.5:1 and is fitted with a twin-choke Weber 32 DIR carburettor

810-06 – 1289 cc engine fitted to automatic-transmission models. Its specification is the same as that for the 810-05 power unit.

Routine engine maintenance

The jobs described in the following sections are those listed in the maintenance schedule. Engine maintenance, of course, also includes a certain amount of work on the cooling system, the carburettor, the petrol pump and the ignition system. These jobs are dealt with in Chapters 10, 11 and 12.

9.1 Engine lubrication and oil changes

The engine oil has been aptly described as the life-blood of the engine. It therefore pays to use a first-class multigrade oil. The correct grades are given in Chapter 17. Here are some important practical tips –

1 The intervals between oil changes recommended in the maintenance schedule *apply only when a multigrade oil is used, under favourable conditions.* Change the oil more frequently when most of the driving is done in cold weather, or when the car is used for short runs and frequent starts are made from cold, or in hot, dusty conditions. In such cases it is best to change the oil after 2000 miles or, in extreme cases, as frequently as every 1000 miles.

2 The correct oil pressure is given in Chapter 17. If the pressure is appreciably below this figure at normal speeds in top gear, with the engine thoroughly warmed-up, investigation is called for. Running the engine with too low a pressure can result in expensive damage to the crankshaft, main and connecting-rod bearings and other components.

3 An oil-pressure gauge is not provided but the oil-pressure warning lamp in the instrument panel will glow if the oil pressure should fall below a safe minimum figure. If the lamp does not light up when the ignition is switched on or does not go out when the engine is running, check the switch on the cylinder block which is operated by the oil pressure. Either fit a replacement switch, or ask a garage to check the oil pressure by temporarily connecting a gauge to the switch union.

4 The sump should be drained when the car has just come in from a run, when the oil is hot and fluid. The system should *not* be flushed out after draining the oil. The drain plug has a 10 mm square recess in it. The

squared end of the special Renault combination spanner B. Vi.380-01 fits the recess and the socket at the other end of the spanner can be used to undo the gearbox drain and level plugs.

However, a practical owner could make a spanner from a length of 10 mm square steel bar. or file a square on the end of a bolt and use a spanner to turn the bolt. Since the gearbox plugs can be undone with an adjustable spanner, the Renault tool is not essential, but is worth having.

9.2 Changing the oil filter element

A full-flow oil filter is provided. This must be renewed after it has been in use for 6000 miles. Carbon, sludge and grit accumulate in the filter, and if the element becomes clogged, a safety valve opens in order to maintain adequate oil circulation to the engine – *but this oil will not be filtered.*

The rubber seal tends to stick to the cylinder block and may be difficult to unscrew. Use a strap-wrench (available from Halfords and other accessory shops) or the Renault tool Mot. 445 to free it.

Sometimes the filter adaptor partially unscrews as the filter is being removed, so before fitting the new filter check that the adaptor is screwed tightly home. The easiest way to tighten it is to use two nuts, one locked against the other. Failure to do this could result in the relief valve in the new filter being held open, allowing unfiltered oil to reach the oilways.

To renew the filter –

Materials: New filter cartridge.
Tools: Strap wrench or special tool Mot. 445.

1 Drain the oil (Section 9.1).

2 Unscrew the filter and discard it.

3 Clean the joint face on the cylinder block and smear the joint ring on the new filter with clean engine oil.

4 Screw the filter into position until it just touches the joint face on the cylinder block. Then screw it by a further quarter-turn, using the strap wrench, slacken it back and finally screw it in by a half to three-quarters of a turn.

5 Refill the sump, run the engine and check for oil leakage past the filter joint when the engine is hot.

9.3 Checking and adjusting the valve clearances

To keep your engine in good tune, check the valve

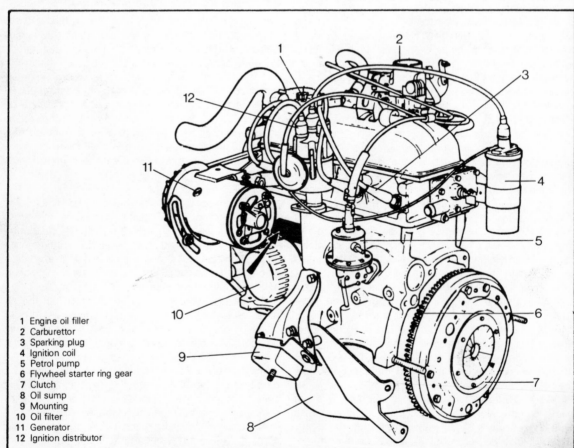

1 Engine oil filler
2 Carburettor
3 Sparking plug
4 Ignition coil
5 Petrol pump
6 Flywheel starter ring gear
7 Clutch
8 Oil sump
9 Mounting
10 Oil filter
11 Generator
12 Ignition distributor

Fig. 9.1 Engine maintenance points. The arrow above item 10 indicates the position of the engine identification plate.

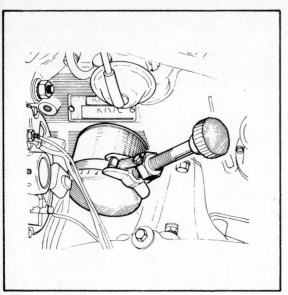

Fig. 9.2 A strap wrench can be used to remove a tight oil filter.

rocker clearances (see below) at 6000-mile intervals. If there is noticeable tapping or clicking from the valve cover on the top of the engine, however, or if the car seems to lack power or liveliness, the rocker clearances should be checked at once, without waiting for the routine service to fall due.

The clearance must also be reset whenever the cylinder-head nuts are tightened down, as this compresses the cylinder-head gasket and the resulting movement of the cylinder head reduces the valve clearances.

The adjusting screws on these engines are not slotted to take a screwdriver blade but have parallel flats machined on them. A smaller spanner or an adjustable may be used to turn them, or a tool can be made up by partly flattening a piece of tube so that it grips the flats. The most satisfactory method, however, is to use the Renault adjusting tool which combines a spanner to fit the lock-nut, with a socket of the correct shape to take the adjusting screw. Make sure that you get the correct wrench. There are different types to suit the various engines. You will also need a set of feeler gauges.

Methods of turning the engine when adjusting the clearances are described on page 16. Renault mechanics sometimes use a remote-control button for the starter switch which allows them to turn the engine over with the sparking plugs installed (but not firing) while the operation of the valves is watched. If the engine is in good condition, after using the starter in this way the crankshaft will come to rest with the exhaust valve of one of the cylinders open. Each exhaust valve can thus be opened in succession and the valve clearances can be checked as described below.

This table should also be used when the engine is rotated by the more conventional methods described on page 16. No. 1 cylinder is that nearest the gearbox. Valve clearances, hot or cold, are given in Chapter 17.

Exhaust valve fully open	Check/adjust clearances on following valves	
	Inlet	Exhaust
1	3	4
2	1	3
3	4	2
4	2	1

The clearances should be checked *only when the engine is cold* (after standing overnight, for example) *or when it is at its normal running temperature.* Four or five miles on the road should be sufficient to ensure that the temperatures of the cylinder block, cylinder head, valves, push-rods and rocker gear have become stabilized. It is not sufficient just to run the engine for a few minutes in the garage before checking the clearances.

To check and adjust the clearances —

1 Disconnect the breather hose, pipes and cables from the valve cover, unscrew the valve cover retaining nuts and lift off the cover.

2 To check the clearances, slide a feeler gauge between the end of the rocker and the tip of the valve stem. It should be a light drag fit – not too loose nor too tight.

3 If adjustment is needed, slacken the lock-nut at the push-rod end of the rocker (preferably use a ring spanner, as the edges of the flats on the nut can easily be burred-over by an open-jawed spanner). Turn the adjusting screw until the correct clearance is obtained and hold it in this position while tightening the lock-nut.

4 Recheck the clearance, which will probably have altered during the first attempt at tightening the lock-nut.

Fig. 9.3 Adjusting the valve clearances. The adjusting screw 1 can be turned after slackening the lock-nut 2. A special tool 3 is not essential but speeds-up the job.

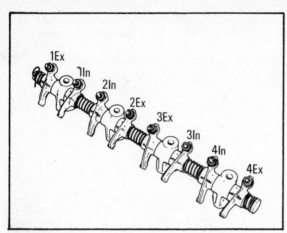

Fig. 9.4 The order in which the inlet and exhaust valve rockers are arranged.

5 Replace the valve-rocker cover. Make sure that the gasket is correctly fitted and tighten the screws evenly. Check for an oil leak after the engine has been run. If necessary reset the automatic governor (Chapter 13, Section 13.11).

9.4 Servicing the crankcase ventilation system

The crankcase fumes are drawn into the inlet manifold and also directly into the carburettor. The breather hose is connected to a gauze flame trap which is fitted to the valve rocker cover.

The amount of air which enters the 810-02 engine is regulated by a calibrated jet, 1.5 mm (0.059 in.) in diameter, which is fitted either in the end of the hose where it is attached to the manifold or close to the carburettor.

On 810-05 and 06 engines two calibrated jets are used, one – 1.5 mm (0.059 in.) diameter – fitted at the carburettor end of the smaller-diameter hose and the other – 6.5 mm (0.256 in.) – in the end of the larger-diameter hose, next to the flame trap.

The jets must be kept clean, to maintain adequate ventilation of the engine, Don't forget to remove them from the old hoses and fit them to the new ones when changing the ventilation hoses.

Engine overhauls

As indicated at the beginning of this chapter, a surprisingly large amount of work can be done without removing the engine from the car. Owing to the use of light alloys for the cylinder head and crankcase and other specialized features of the engine, such as the fitting of removable 'wet' cylinder barrels, however, the use of special Renault tools is advisable for some jobs.

In some cases we suggest alternative ways of doing the work but where we recommend that a special tool should be used, it would be unwise to adopt makeshift methods unless this cannot be avoided.

It is also essential to quote the chassis number and the engine type and number of your car when ordering spares. A number of modifications have been introduced over the years and in some cases only the new type of component is available as a spare. This may mean that suitably modified parts must also be used with the new unit.

It must be assumed, of course, that if you are prepared to tackle major overhauls you will have had some experience of engine dismantling, fitting and assembly, or will be able to rely on the help of a knowledgeable friend.

The time factor

It is not always easy to estimate the time required for engine overhaul jobs, since so much depends on the facilities available. The following times, however, are suggested for typical jobs: Partial engine overhaul (see Chapter 8), 2-3 days; top-overhaul and decarbonizing, allow at least one full day – preferably a week-end; removing and refitting engine, 10-1.1 hr.

Decarbonizing and top-overhaul

Removal of the cylinder head, cleaning off deposits of carbon and reseating the valves is usually termed 'decarbonizing', although a more correct term, in view of the work involved, is a 'top-overhaul'.

If the job is confined solely to removing and refitting the head – to replace a faulty gasket, for example – only the appropriate sections apply.

The lists of materials and tools required which follow cover a complete top-overhaul, but can, of course, be modified to suit the actual stages carried out.

Materials: Gasket set. Water hoses. Set of valve springs. Spare exhaust valves (have at least two in reserve as a safety margin). Magnus Magstrip liquid (from a Renault dealer). Valve-grinding paste. Emery paper. Rags. Paraffin. Tins, jars, boxes for parts.
Tools: Set of spanners. Socket spanners. Screwdrivers. Pliers. Plastic-faced mallet. Blunt scraper for carbon. Wire brush. Valve-spring compressor. Torque wrench. Syringe or plastic tube. Straightedge. Feeler gauges. Electric drill with wire brushes – desirable but not essential.

9.5 Removing the cylinder head

The following points are vitally important when removing the cylinder head, in view of the use of light-alloys in the head and cylinder block, and the installation of removable cylinder barrels.

The cylinder-head bolts must be slackened progressively in the opposite sequence to that shown in Fig. 9.5 and must be undone only when the head is cold, in order to avoid distortion of the head.

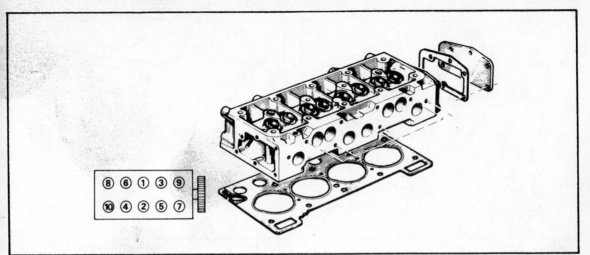

Fig. 9.5 The cylinder head and gasket. The bolts must be tightened progressively in the order shown.

If the engine is rotated while the cylinder head is off, the friction between the piston rings and the cylinder barrels may lift the barrels and disturb their seals. This can be avoided by clamping the flanges of the barrels down, using short strips of metal, drilled to take a cylinder-head bolt and held in place by screwing the bolts into the cylinder block with suitable distance pieces between the heads of the bolts and the strips. Renault dealers use the more sophisticated liner clamp (Mot. 521) shown in Fig. 9.6.

A metal scraper must never be used to remove any traces of gasket from the head and block. Magnus Magstrip liquid (obtainable from a Renault dealer) should be painted on the seating faces and left for about 10 minutes to dissolve the remnants of gasket, which can then be cleaned off with a sharpened piece of wood. Wear rubber gloves when doing this, and do not allow the liquid to drip on to the paintwork.

Materials and tools: see page 40

1 Begin by disconnecting the battery, draining the cooling system (Chapter 10) and taking off the air filter.

2 Next disconnect the wires, cables and hoses from the carburettor, alternator, ignition distributor and the cylinder head.

3 Slacken the alternator strut adjustment, remove the belt and take off the alternator.

4 Remove the ignition distributor (Chapter 12).

5 Take off the valve cover. The sparking plug wrench fits the retaining nuts.

6 Disconnect the exhaust downpipe from the manifold and from the side stiffener and also disconnect the hot-air take-off pipe and the brake servo vacuum pipe, when these items are fitted.

7 Slacken the cylinder head bolts progressively in the reverse order to that shown in Fig. 9.5. It is very important to slacken each bolt only a little at a time, to avoid any risk of distorting the cylinder head.

8 Take out the cylinder head bolts and free the head from the gasket. If it sticks, turn the engine over with the starter. Provided that the sparking plugs have not been removed the engine compression should be sufficient to break the joint.

9 Lift the head slightly to disengage the push-rods from the rockers and remove each push-rod, giving it a sharp twist with the fingers to break the suction of the oil at its lower end, to avoid disturbing the cam followers. As each rod is withdrawn, place it in a safe place in the correct order, so that it can be refitted in its original position.

10 Carefully lift off the cylinder head and do not rotate the engine until liner clamps have been fitted as described at the beginning of this section.

9.6 Dismantling the cylinder head

Materials and tools: see page 40

If you do not intend to carry out a top-overhaul — for example, if the only reason for removing the cylinder head is to renew a faulty cylinder-head gasket — the combustion chambers can be decarbonized without further dismantling, although it is better to remove the manifolds to allow the inlet and exhaust ports to be cleaned out. In any event, it is best to decarbonize the combustion chambers before removing the valves, to avoid the risk of damaging the valve seatings in the cylinder head.

During a top-overhaul, of course, it will be necessary to remove the valves for inspection and refacing of the valves and seatings, or renewal of any valves which are in too poor condition to justify refacing and refitting them.

To dismantle the cylinder head —

1 Remove the fan and the water pump, the inlet and exhaust manifold, together with the carburettor hoses, and the end-plate from the head.

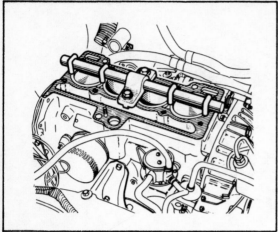

Fig. 9.6 The Renault cylinder-barrel clamp which prevents movement of the barrels when the engine is rotated with the head removed.

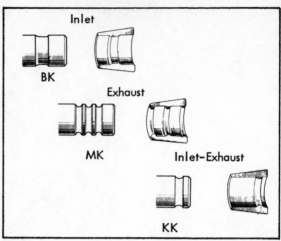

Fig. 9.7 The various types of valve-stem collets which have been fitted. The BK and MK patterns are earlier types, superseded by the KK pattern.

2 Take off the inlet and exhaust manifolds if this has not been done previously. The carburettor can be left on the inlet manifold.

3 Remove the valves, as described in Section 9.8; but if the cylinder head is to be decarbonized, defer removing the valves until the combustion chambers have been cleaned (see below).

9.7 Decarbonizing the cylinder head

Materials and tools: see page 40

1 Decarbonize the combustion-chamber faces before removing the valves, to avoid any risk of damaging the valve seatings. Scrape off every trace of carbon.

2 Thoroughly clean the cylinder-block and manifold mating faces of the head, taking particular care not to score them. Use Magnus Magstrip liquid to dissolve remnants of gasket as described in Section 9.5.

9.8 Removing and cleaning the valves

The valve-spring caps are retained by split-cone collets and a valve-spring compressor is needed to remove them.

Fit a set of new valve springs (tired springs will undo most of the benefit that should be obtained from a top overhaul).

If you are fitting new valves or collets, make sure that the pattern of the ridges on the inside of the collets matches the grooves in the valve stem. There are several alternative arrangements of the grooves, and also the inlet and exhaust valve patterns may be different.

Materials and tools: see page 40

1 Remove the rocker shaft, take off the clips and slide the rockers, springs and pillars off the shaft, being careful to keep all the parts in their correct sequence. Check the fit of each rocker on its original position on the shaft and if it is sloppy, recheck its fit on an unworn section of the shaft. This will enable you to decide whether a new

set of rockers, or new rockers and a new shaft will be needed. If the noses of the rockers are badly indented where they rest on the tips of the valve stems, it may not be sufficient simply to grind off the protruding metal. The case-hardened skin may have been pierced and again new rockers will be needed.

2 Compress each valve spring with the spring-compressor until the spring cap is clear of the split collets. Remove these and release the spring.

3 Take off the valve-spring retainer, sleeve and spring. Draw the valve out of its guide.

4 Clean the undersides of the valve heads, the stems and also the ports in the head which could not be reached when the valves were in position. Be careful not to score the faces of the valves and their seats in the combustion chambers. Wire-wool soap-pads quickly remove carbon.

5 Scrape the valve stems clean. Don't use emery cloth on the sections that work in the guides. Clean out the guides themselves by drawing a paraffin-soaked rag through them.

6 Check each valve for fit in its own guide. If there is any noticeable degree of sideways shake, take the head to your dealer for advice. If he confirms that the valves and guides are worn, allow him to renew the guides, to recut the seats in the head and to fit new valves.

9.9 Valve grinding

If the seating faces on the exhaust valves are badly pitted, they can be trued-up by using a valve refacing tool (your garage should be able to do this for you).

Badly-pitted valve seatings in the cylinder head can be refaced with a special tool — normally this is also a job for your garage. If the pitting is only slight, however, the valves can be ground-in in the conventional manner, as described below.

The object of grinding-in the valves (or more correctly,

lapping-in) is to obtain a gastight seal between each valve and its seating. The importance of making a really good job of valve-lapping cannot be over-emphasized, since not only the cylinder compressions but the service life of the valves will depend on a first-class seal between the valves and their seatings.

Valve-grinding paste usually comes in a tin which contains two grades, fine and coarse. The coarse paste should be used only in an emergency, to remove pitting when proper reconditioning cannot be carried out, but light pitting may be removed with the fine paste, grinding being continued until a good matt finish has been obtained on the valve and seat.

Materials and tools: see page 40

1 Smear a little grinding-paste on the face of the valve and rotate the valve quickly and lightly on its seat with the suction-cup grinding tool, first in one direction and then in the other, by spinning the handle of the tool between the palms of the hands. From time to time, raise the valve from its seat and turn it through a quarter of a turn, before continuing the grinding. This will ensure that an even, concentric surface is obtained. A light coil spring, placed beneath the head of the valve, will make the job easier, as it will lift the valve whenever pressure on it is relaxed.

2 Check the progress of the grinding-in frequently. When correctly ground, both the valve seat in the cylinder head and the face of the valve should have an even, clean, grey matt finish with no signs of bright rings or any evidence of pitting. Bright rings are caused by grinding with insufficient grinding paste, while 'tramlines' are usually the result of continuously grinding the valve on its seat without taking up a different position.

3 Check the effectiveness of the seal by making a series of pencil marks across the face of the valve with a soft lead pencil. Replace the valve and rotate it once through a quarter of a turn on its seat. Each pencil mark should be erased at the line of contact. If any of the lines are unbroken, either the valve or its seat is not truly circular and renewal or refacing of the valve or seat (or both) is required.

9.10 Reassembling the valves

Materials and tools: see page 40

1 When the valves have been ground-in, wash them and their seats in the cylinder head with petrol or paraffin, making sure that all traces of valve-grinding paste have been removed. Lubricate the valve stems and the guides with engine oil.

2 When refitting the springs, cups and collets note, as

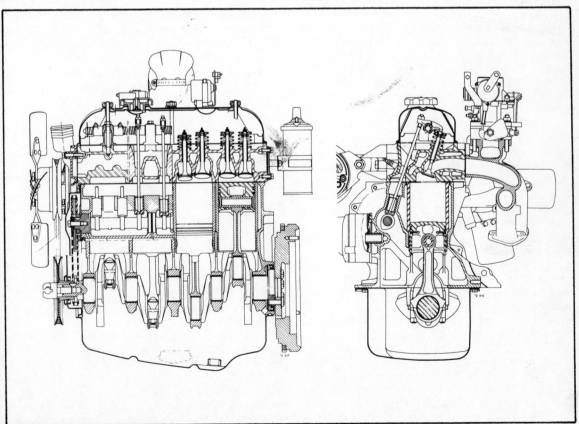

Fig. 9.8 Longitudinal and vertical sections through the engine.

already mentioned, that three different types of collets have been used. These are shown in Fig. 9.7 and it is important to match the collet to the groove on the valve stem. The most closely-spaced coils of the springs must be towards the cylinder head.

3 When assembling the rockers and the rocker shaft, the holes in the shaft must be lined-up with those in the pillars.

9.11 Decarbonizing the pistons

Materials and tools: see page 40

1 Rotate the crankshaft until two of the pistons are at the tops of the cylinders. Clamps *must* be fitted to the cylinder barrels to prevent them being disturbed – see Section 9.5.

2 Stuff clean rags into the bores of the remaining cylinders and in the water-ways and other openings in the cylinder block.

3 Remove the carbon from the piston crowns with a suitable blunt scraper, taking care not to score the surfaces. Then burnish the crowns with a wire brush.

9.12 Refitting the cylinder head

Refitting the cylinder head is largely a reversal of the dismantling process, but the following points are very important –

The cylinder head and block must be scrupulously clean. As recommended earlier, use Magnus Magstrip liquid to dissolve any remnants of gasket. Use a syringe or a length of plastic tube to suck any oil out of the cylinder-head bolt holes in the block. Oil at the bases of the holes will prevent the bolts being tightened down fully.

Check the cylinder head for signs of warping by placing a straightedge across the gasket face of the head in several different positions and measuring the gap, if any, between the head and the straightedge with a feeler gauge. The maximum permissible bow in the head is 0.05 mm (0.002 in.). If the head is distorted, a Renault dealer can probably grind it true, but the maximum amount of metal that can be removed is 0.5 mm (0.02 in.). If this will not remove the distortion a new head must be fitted.

The flanges of the cylinder barrels must protrude slightly above the block to provide the correct 'nip' between the barrels and the gasket when the head is tightened down. Renault dealers use a dial gauge mounted on a special block to check the protrusion, but a straightedge and a feeler gauge will do. Place the straightedge across each barrel in several positions and measure the gap between the underside of the rule and the top of the block. The correct protrusion should be between 0.04-0.012 mm (0.0015-0.005 in.). If the protrusion is incorrect it can be adjusted by fitting a seal of a different thickness to the cylinder barrel – see Section 9.19.

Materials and tools: see page 40

1 Make sure that the locating dowels are in place in the cylinder block.

2 The gaskets for the water pump and the end-plate must be fitted dry, without jointing compound.

3 Also fit the cylinder-head gasket dry and with the HAUT/TOP letters facing upwards

4 Fit the cylinder head, being careful not to disturb the gasket.

5 Wipe the cylinder-head bolts clean, smear their threads and washers lightly with engine oil, screw the bolts in finger-tight and then tighten them *progressively and smoothly (without jerks)* in the order shown in figure 9.5. It is most important to follow the tightening sequence given below in order to avoid distorting the head and to prevent subsequent gasket troubles.

6 Tighten the nuts initially in the correct sequence to 40-50 lb ft (55-65 Nm). When reassembly has been completed *run the engine without load for 10 minutes.* Then switch off, unscrew each nut a quarter of a turn and retighten it to 50 lb ft (65 Nm).

7 Complete the assembly, adjust the valve clearances (Section 9.3), warm up the engine and check the carburettor idling adjustments (Chapter 11) and the ignition timing (Chapter 12). After 300 miles recheck all adjustments.

8 On automatic transmission models it will be necessary to adjust the governor setting (Chapter 13, Section 13.11).

9.13 Fitting a new timing cover oil seal

The oil seal in the timing cover behind the crankshaft pulley can be replaced without the need for removing the engine, but the special Renault tool set Mot.457 should preferably be used to remove the old seal and to fit the new one.

When this set is not available, however, it is possible to do the job at home, provided that great care is taken not to damage the new seal.

Materials: New oil seal. Timing chain cover gasket, if cover is removed. Paraffin. Rags. Engine oil.
Tools: Jack. Axle stands. Spanners, including a well-fitting socket for crankshaft pulley nut or a bar for the starting-handle dog. Gear puller or levers for pulley. Screwdrivers. Hammer and tubular drift. Special tool set Mot.457 (not essential).

1 Slacken the alternator adjustment and remove the driving belt.

2 Jack-up and support the front of the car and unscrew the starting handle dog on an earlier model or the nut which replaces the dog and secures the crankshaft pulley on a later car. When a dog is fitted, a bar must be threaded through the hole in the dog in order to unscrew it. With a nut, a well-fitting socket spanner is essential. In either case the dog or nut is usually very tight and a sharp blow with a hammer will be needed to

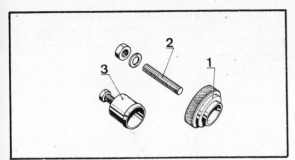

Fig. 9:9 The special tool Mot.457 should preferably be used to change the timing chain cover oil seal. It consists of a centralizing sleeve 1, a threaded rod 2, with nut and washer and an extracting tool, 3.

free it. To prevent the crankshaft rotating, remove the starter motor and lock the flywheel or convertor drive plate by wedging a strong screwdriver between the teeth of the ring gear. Renault dealers have a serrated locking plate which fits the teeth of the ring gear and is bolted in place and obviously if this can be borrowed it will reduce any risk of damaging the gear.

3 An alternative method of freeing the dog or the retaining nut is to wedge the end of the bar or spanner firmly against rotation, disconnect the low-tension lead from the ignition coil to prevent the engine starting and momentarily operate the starter motor. The sudden jerk of the crankshaft should slacken the dog or the nut, which can then be unscrewed by hand.

4 Remove the crankshaft pulley, using a two-legged extractor if it is tight. Alternatively lever carefully behind it with two screwdrivers, being careful not to damage the timing cover.

5 The old oil seal can now be removed either by passing the flange of the extracting tool from the special set behind it and tightening the central screw, or by levering it out carefully with a hooked tool. It does not matter if the old seal is damaged, of course, but the housing must not be scored.

6 Fit the new seal with its lip inwards towards the crankshaft. If the special tool set is being used the seal is simply slipped over the flange of the knurled tool, the threaded rod is screwed into the nose of the crankshaft and the seal is drawn into place by tightening the nut on the rod until the sleeve just touches the crankshaft.

If the tool set is not available, carefully tap the new seal fully home in its housing, using a suitable tubular drift and being very careful to keep the seal square.

7 Examine the section of the pulley boss on which the seal runs and if it is scored or pitted fit a new pulley.

8 If the timing cover has been removed refit it, and the pulley, as described in Section 9.14, items 13 and 14.

9.14 Fitting a new timing chain and sprockets

This job can be done without removing the engine from the car.

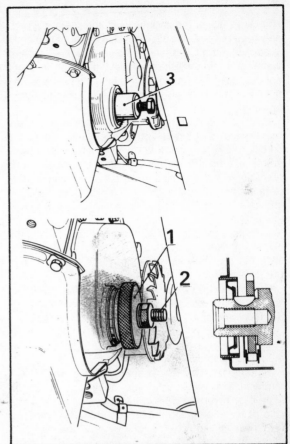

Fig. 9.10 Changing the timing chain cover oil seal. The extractor tool 3 of Mot.457 is used to remove the old seal. The centralizing sleeve 1 positions the new seal and the threaded rod is used with the nut and washer to draw the seal into place.

Materials: New chain, sprockets and tensioner, if required. Gaskets. Thin wire. Paraffin. Engine oil.
Tools: Jack. Axle stands. Spanners. Screwdrivers. Hammer. Tubular drift. Also tools for Sections 9.13 and 9.16

1 Jack-up and support the front of the car and remove the alternator, fan and pulley, engine dephaser, the crankshaft pulley (Section 9.13) and the oil sump (Section 9.16).

2 Take off the timing cover.

3 Remove the chain tensioner. If this is of the manual initial take-up type, unscrew the plug from the outer end of the tensioner, insert a 3 mm hexagonal Allen key and turn the key clockwise. If the tensioner is of the automatic take-up type, keep the pad in place by binding a short length of wire around it before removing the tensioner retaining bolts.

4 Unlock and unscrew the camshaft sprocket retaining bolt and ease off the camshaft sprocket and the chain. If necessary, carefully apply leverage behind the sprocket with two screwdrivers.

5 Examine the teeth of the camshaft and crankshaft sprockets. When the chain is worn the teeth will probably have developed a slightly 'hooked' formation and it is advisable to fit new sprockets when a new chain is installed. If the crankshaft sprocket is a tight fit, a suitable two-legged extractor should be used to remove it – but again, most owners would probably resort to careful levering.

6 When reassembling, it will be necessary to expand the bore of the crankshaft sprocket by heating the sprocket in boiling water before it is tapped into place with a tubular drift. Then fit the camshaft sprocket with the V timing mark facing outwards, turn the camshaft to align this mark with the V on the crankshaft sprocket, as shown in Fig. 9.11, using a straightedge or a length of string.

7 Remove the camshaft sprocket without turning the camshaft, fit the timing chain to both sprockets and slide the camshaft sprocket into place, checking that the timing marks are still aligned.

8 Fit the locking plate, screw in the camshaft sprocket bolt, tighten it to the correct torque and lock it.

9 Clean the chain tensioner filter and install it.

10 If the tensioner is of the automatic take-up type, and the pad has been wired back, fit the tensioner and then remove the wire.

11 If the tensioner has been dismantled while it was removed, lock the piston in the shoe, using a 3 mm Allen key, insert the shoe in the body and place a thin strip of metal between the shoe and the body to prevent the tensioner expanding. Fit the tensioner and then remove the metal strip, press the shoe inwards until the piston touches the bottom of the body and allow the pad to move outwards without assisting the action of the spring.

12 After fitting a manually-adjusted tensioner, turn the Allen key clockwise until the pad is in contact with the chain, remove the key and fit and lock the cylinder retaining bolt.

13 When refitting the timing cover, use a new gasket and leave the retaining nuts and bolts finger-tight until the crankshaft pulley has been eased into place, thus centralizing the seal in the cover around the hub of the pulley. Lubricate the hub of the pulley generously with engine oil and rotate it as it is inserted to prevent any risk of damaging the delicate lip of the seal. The keyway in the pulley must line-up with the key in the crankshaft before the pulley is finally tapped home.

14 When tightening the cover nuts and bolts be careful not to disturb the position of the cover and do not overtighten them, as this may distort the flange of the cover and cause an oil leak.

15 The remainder of reassembling is a reversal of dismantling, any special points being covered in the appropriate sections of this chapter.

9.15 Removing and refitting the camshaft

To remove and refit the camshaft the engine must be taken out of the car, but fortunately this job is only likely to be done when the engine is being overhauled. The Renault 12 power unit does not normally suffer from excessive wear of the cams or the camshaft bearings.

If a new camshaft is being fitted, it is advisable to renew the tappets – also known as the cam followers – at the same time.

To remove and refit the shaft –

Materials and tools: As listed in the various sections covering the steps in dismantling described below.

1 Remove the engine, take off the cylinder head,

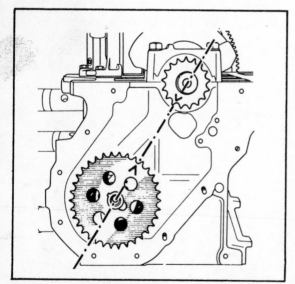

Fig. 9.11 The 'V' timing marks on the crankshaft and camshaft sprockets must be aligned as shown.

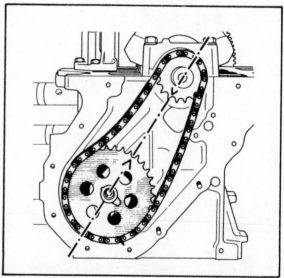

Fig. 9.12 When the chain is fitted and the camshaft sprockets slid into place, check that the reference marks are still in line.

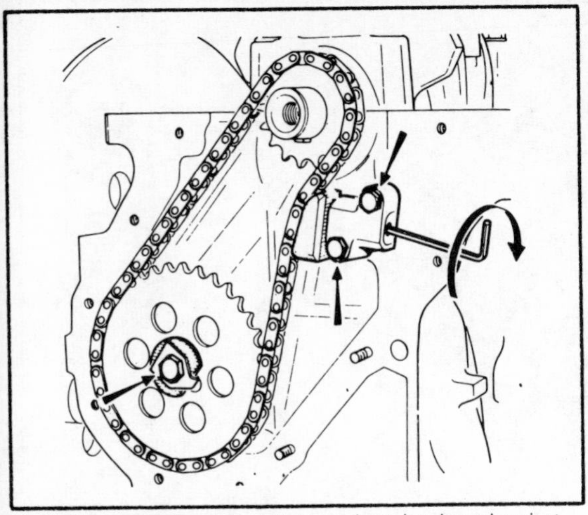

remove the push-rods and fit clamps to the cylinder barrels (Sections 9.21/22 and 9.5).

2 Remove the oil sump and the oil pump (Sections 9.16 and 9.17) and the tappet blocks, keeping the tappets in the original order if they are to be refitted.

3 Remove the distributor and the distributor driving shaft (Section 9.18).

4 Remove the timing chain cover, chain tensioner, chain and camshaft sprocket (Sections 9.13 and 9.14).

5 Unscrew the setscrews which secure the camshaft retaining flange and carefully withdraw the shaft.

6 Examine the cams for signs of scoring, pitting or excessive wear and if in doubt fit a new camshaft and a set of tappets. Renewing the components separately will only result in excessive wear of the new parts.

7 Using a feeler gauge, measure the clearance between the back of the retaining flange and the boss on the camshaft after temporarily refitting the sprocket and tightening the sprocket bolt to a torque of 20 lb ft (30 Nm). The correct clearance is 0.002-0.005 in. (0.06-0.11 mm). If the clearance is too great it will be necessary to fit a new flange and since a press must be used for this job, it is better to leave it to a Renault dealer.

8 When refitting the camshaft, sprockets, chain and tensioner, follow the sequence given in Sections 9.13 and 9.14.

9.16 Removing and refitting the oil sump

Materials: Paraffin. Clean cloth. Soft bristle brush.
Tools: Jack. Axle stands. Spanners. Screwdriver. Four sump-locating studs – these can be made by cutting the heads off spare sump-retaining bolts and slotting the ends to take a screwdriver.

1 If the engine has not been removed, it will be necessary to drain the sump, remove the dephaser, release the anti-roll bar brackets on the side members and lower the bar before the sump can be withdrawn.

2 Clean the sludge out of the sump, using paraffin, a brush and a clean cloth. Also clean the gauze filter on the oil pump but be careful not to damage the mesh. *Do not leave any threads or lint from the cloth in the sump or on the gauze.*

3 Before refitting the sump, carefully clean the flanges and check that they have not been distorted by overtightening of the retaining bolts.

4 Fit a new gasket and new main bearing rubber seals.

5 Smear the ends of the side gaskets with gasket jointing compound and make sure that their ends overlap the rubber seals.

6 Retain each gasket in place by screwing a locating stud – see 'Tools' – into each corner of the cylinder block.

7 Fit the sump, being careful not to disturb the gaskets, screw in the bolts finger-tight, remove the studs and replace them by bolts, and then tighten the bolts

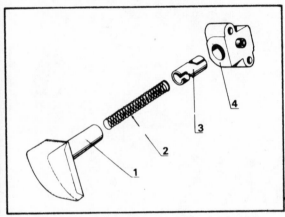

Fig. 9.13 A manually-adjusted chain tensioner is released against the chain by turning an Allen key in the direction shown. The nuts indicated by the arrows must be securely tightened.

Fig. 9.14 An automatic chain tensioner consists of a shoe 1, a spring 2, a piston 3 and the tensioner body 4.

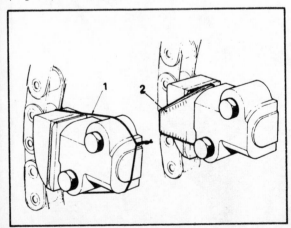

Fig. 9.15 An automatic chain tensioner should be wired (1) before removing it. If it has been dismantled a strip of metal or card (or the plastic keep 2 supplied with the new tensioner) should be installed to retain the piston while fitting the tensioner.

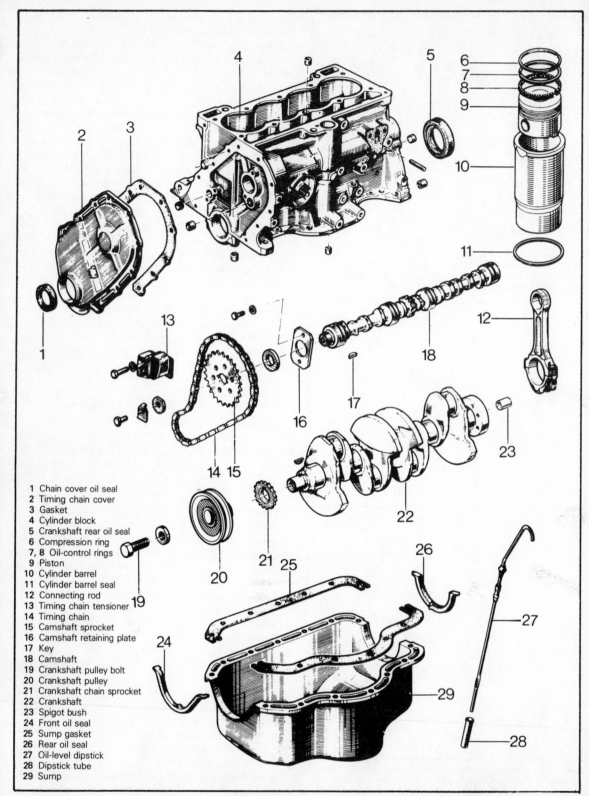

1 Chain cover oil seal
2 Timing chain cover
3 Gasket
4 Cylinder block
5 Crankshaft rear oil seal
6 Compression ring
7, 8 Oil-control rings
9 Piston
10 Cylinder barrel
11 Cylinder barrel seal
12 Connecting rod
13 Timing chain tensioner
14 Timing chain
15 Camshaft sprocket
16 Camshaft retaining plate
17 Key
18 Camshaft
19 Crankshaft pulley bolt
20 Crankshaft pulley
21 Crankshaft chain sprocket
22 Crankshaft
23 Spigot bush
24 Front oil seal
25 Sump gasket
26 Rear oil seal
27 Oil-level dipstick
28 Dipstick tube
29 Sump

Fig. 9.16 The 'bottom half' engine components dismantled.

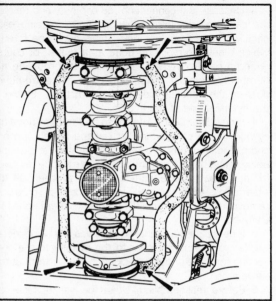

Fig. 9.17 When fitting the oil sump, temporary locating studs (shown by the arrows) should be used to position the sump gaskets.

evenly and progressively to avoid distorting the sump flanges.

9.17 The oil pump, pressure-relief valve and suction filter

These items can be reached by raising the car and dropping the sump as described in Section 9.16. The oil pump can then be taken off by removing the three securing bolts.

Do not fit a gasket between the pump and the cylinder block when refitting the pump.

1 The pump gears and the pressure-relief valve ball and spring can be inspected after the pump cover has been taken off. Be careful not to allow the ball and spring to fly out while removing the cover.

2 The end-play between the gears and the pump body should not exceed 0.008 in. (0.2 mm). If the clearance is excessive, new gears can be fitted. It is also advisable to fit a new relief-valve spring, as the valve is not adjustable.

3 Apart from a worn pump, low oil pressure can be caused by general wear throughout the engine. In such cases even a new oil pump will not restore the full running pressure and a complete engine overhaul will be needed – or at least attention to the main and connecting-rod big-end bearings.

9.18 Removing and refitting the ignition distributor driving shaft

The ignition distributor is driven by a vertical shaft, fitted at its upper end with an offset driving dog which ensures the correct ignition timing when the distributor is removed and refitted as described in Chapter 12. The

shaft is driven by a skew gear at the centre of the camshaft and beneath this gear there is a splined drive for the shaft of the oil pump.

To remove and refit the driving shaft –

Tools: Spanners. Special tool Ele.556 (not essential). Bolt, 12 mm diameter with 175 pitch thread.

1 Remove the distributor as described in Chapter 12. The special tool Ele.556 makes it easier to unscrew the retaining bolt.

2 Screw a 12 mm diameter bolt which has a 175 pitch thread into the upper end of the driving shaft and withdraw the shaft.

3 When refitting the shaft turn the crankshaft to bring No. 1 piston to top-dead-centre on the compression stroke, with both valves closed and the timing mark aligned as described in Chapter 12, Section 12.12.

4 The shaft will rotate as the gear on it engages with the gear on the camshaft. It should come to rest with the driving slot at right-angles to the centre line of the engine, and with the largest 'D' towards the rear of the engine as shown in Fig. 9.19. If necessary withdraw the gear and turn it slightly so that the drive is correctly positioned when it is fully home.

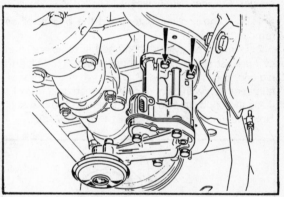

Fig. 9.18 The oil pump is accessible when the sump has been removed. Two of the three locating screws are shown by the arrows.

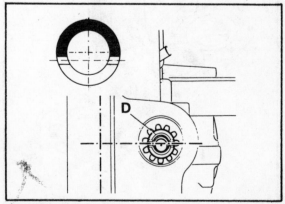

Fig. 9.19 Installing the distributor and oil-pump driving shaft. With the shaft fully home the driving slot should be in the position shown, with the largest D towards the rear of the engine.

9.19 Changing the cylinder barrels, pistons and connecting-rod bearing shells

New cylinder barrels and pistons are supplied in a 'liner-piston' kit, the barrels, pistons, piston rings and gudgeon pins being in matched sets. Mark the parts in each box with the cylinder numbers 1 to 4 (No. 1 is at the flywheel end) as soon as they have been upacked, so that there is no risk of mixing them. The anti-rust coating should be wiped off with a solvent such as petrol just before use. Do not scrape the parts clean.

The gudgeon pins are a sliding fit in the pistons and an interference fit in the connecting-rod small-ends. As the ends of the rods must be heated to 250°C (482°F) to allow the new pins to be fitted, and a set of special tools, consisting of piston thrust pads, assembly mandrels, guides and a support base for the piston should be used in conjunction with an arbor press to fit the new pins, it is advisable to let your dealer carry out this work.

Materials: Any new parts required, including new cylinder-barrel seals of correct thickness. Marking paint. Magnus Magstrip liquid. Paraffin. Rags. Engine oil.

Tools: Spanners and sockets. Torque wrench. Hammer. Soft-faced mallet. Centre-punch. Straightedge. Feeler gauges. Cylinder-barrel clamps.

1 Drain the cooling system and the engine oil and remove the sump.

2 Take off the cylinder head and fit retainers to the cylinder barrels as described in Section 9.5. Wipe the big-end caps clean and if they are not numbered, number them with paint or centre-punch dots from 1 to 4, on the opposite side of the engine to the camshaft, No. 1 bearing being that nearest to the flywheel.

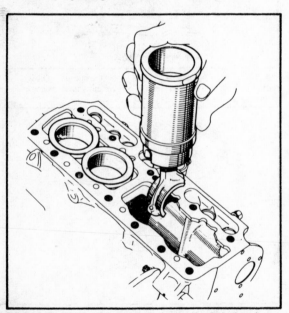

Fig. 9.20 Installing a connecting-rod, piston and cylinder barrel assembly in the cylinder block.

3 Unscrew the connecting-rod cap nuts and take off the caps and the lower bearing shells, keeping each shell with its cap unless new shells are to be fitted – which would normally be done as a matter of course during a partial overhaul. If the caps and rods are not numbered, number them with paint or centre-punch dots on the opposite side to the camshaft, starting at the flywheel end of the engine.

4 If new liner-piston kits are to be fitted, remove the cylinder barrel clamps and lift out the barrels, pistons and connecting rods as assemblies. If new parts are not being fitted, but the pistons and liners must be removed for any reason, take particular care to keep all the assemblies together and in the correct order as removed from the engine. Don't disturb them unnecessarily.

5 If new piston and liner assemblies are being installed, let your Renault dealer fit the pistons to the connecting rods. He should check each rod for truth at the same time.

6 Before reassembling, clean the gasket faces on the cylinder head and block with Magnus Magstrip liquid (see Section 9.5). Also clean the locations for the cylinder barrels inside the block – *but do not scrape them clean.*

7 Fit a seal with a blue colour code to each cylinder barrel, insert the barrel in its correct position, press it down firmly by hand and check the protrusion above the face of the cylinder block as described in Section 9.12. If the protrusion is incorrect, try fitting a seal of a different thickness. A blue colour code indicates a seal which is 0.08 mm (0.0032 in.) thick. A red seal is 0.1 mm (0.004 in.) thick and a green seal 0.12 mm (0.005 in.) thick. If the correct protrusion cannot be obtained with any of these seals, the fault may lie in the crankcase and the advice of your Renault dealer should be sought.

8 Remove the cylinder barrels from the block and fit each piston and connecting-rod assembly to its own barrel, using a suitable piston-ring clamp. Oil the barrels, rings and pistons before assembly, turn the rings so that their gaps are spaced equally around the piston and check that the arrow on each piston crown faces towards the flywheel and that the numbers on the connecting rods and caps are on the side opposite to the camshaft. The machined side of each big-end must be parallel to the flats on top of the liner.

9 Fit the correct thickness of seal, as determined earlier, to each cylinder barrel. Fit the upper halves of the shell bearings to the connecting rods and install the barrel assemblies in the crankcase. Fit the barrel clamps.

10 Lubricate the crankpins and pull the connecting rods down on to them. Fit the bearing shells in the big-end caps and install the caps, tightening the nuts to the correct torque (Chapter 17).

11 Rotate the crankshaft to make sure that the bearings are not binding.

9.20 Removing, servicing and refitting the crank-shaft and main bearings

If the crankshaft is simply being removed and refitted during engine dismantling, and it is not intended to renew the main-bearing shells (although this would, of course, normally be done if the engine had covered more than 20 000-30 000 miles), check the crankshaft end-play before removing the bearing caps.

Insert a feeler gauge beside one of the thrust washers at the centre bearing and prise the crankshaft in each direction.

The maximum permissible movement is 0.05-0.23 mm (0.002-0.009 in.). This is controlled by thrust washers which are available in 2.28 mm (0.09 in.), 2.38 mm (0.094 in.) and 2.43 mm (0.096 in.) thicknesses. The correct end-float can be obtained by selecting the appropriate washers.

The flywheel or converter drive plate retaining bolts are self-locking and new bolts must be fitted whenever the flywheel is removed.

To remove and refit the crankshaft and bearings and to fit new bearing shells if necessary –

Materials: Any new parts required. Paraffin. Rags. Marking paint. Engine oil.

Tools: Spanners. Sockets. Torque wrench. Hammer. Soft-faced mallet. Centre-punch. Feeler gauges. Locating studs for bearing cap – see item 14. Special tool Mot. 131-02 – see item 12. Syringe.

1 Remove the flywheel or the converter driving plate by unscrewing the retaining bolts.

2 Number the bearing caps on the opposite side of the engine to the camshaft with paint or centre-punch dots if this has not already been done, starting at the flywheel end.

3 Undo and remove the bearing caps complete with their shells.

4 Remove the oil seal from No. 1 bearing.

5 Lift out the crankshaft and take out the bearing shells from the crankcase. Also remove the thrust washers. If the bearings are to be re-used, it is important to keep each pair with its bearing cap so that they can be fitted in the original positions.

6 Make sure that the crankshaft oilways are clear by flushing them with paraffin from a syringe, followed by clean engine oil.

7 The bush in the end of the crankshaft, which locates the gearbox input shaft, should be renewed. It can be withdrawn by screwing a thread tap into it and pulling on the shank of the tap, or by partly filling the recess with grease, inserting a closely-fitting bar, or even a hardwood dowel, and giving the end of the bar a sharp tap with a hammer. The hydraulic pressure will then eject the bush. When fitting the new bush, use a suitable tubular drift and be very careful to insert the bush squarely and not to burr the internal bore.

8 When reassembling, fit the upper sections of the bearing shells into the crankcase. These are the halves which have oil feed holes and grooves. The tags must locate in the cut-outs. Smear the thrust washers with grease to hold them in position and insert them. The sides which are faced with anti-friction metal must face the crankshaft webs.

9 Lubricate the shells and the crankshaft journals with engine oil and lower the crankshaft into position.

10 Fit the bearing shells into the bearing caps.

11 All the cap bolts can now be tightened progressively to 40-50 lb ft (55-65 Nm). When this has been done, check that the crankshaft still rotates freely and also that the end-play is correct.

12 A new oil seal should now be fitted to the bearing at the flywheel end. Officially the special tool Mot.131-02 should be used. If this is not available, great care must be taken when installing the seal as its lip is very delicate. Lubricate the lip with engine oil, partly insert the seal by hand, and use a piece of tubing of suitable

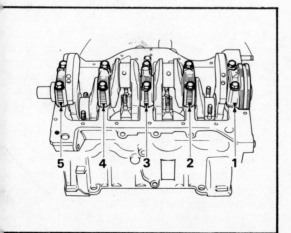

Fig. 9.21 The crankshaft main bearing caps should be numbered on the opposite side to the camshaft, beginning from the flywheel end of the engine.

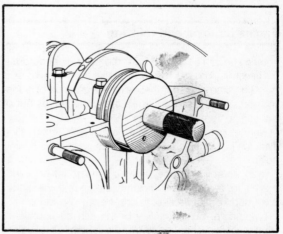

Fig. 9.22 If the special tool Mot.131-02 is available, it should be used to fit the rear crankshaft oil seal.

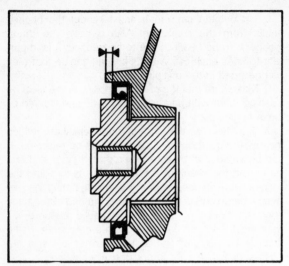

Fig. 9.23 The rear crankshaft oil seal should be moved inwards as shown to the extent of 3 mm (⅛ in.), if the original crankshaft is being refitted.

diameter, or the base of a suitably-sized tin, to press it into place. If the original crankshaft is being re-used, position the seal 3 mm (⅛ in.) inside the outer edge of its housing so that it will not be bearing on the same section of the crankshaft as the old seal. If a new or a reground crankshaft has been fitted, fit the seal with its outer face flush with the outer edge of the housing.

13 Inspect the flywheel for scores caused by a worn clutch lining. If these are bad it will be necessary to fit a new flywheel, or to ask your Renault dealer whether he can reface the old one. If the starter ring gear is badly worn, a new flywheel must be fitted, as starter rings are not supplied as separate parts. If a converter drive plate is fitted instead of a flywheel, the ring gear will be welded in place and a new drive plate must be installed if the teeth of the ring are worn. When refitting the flywheel or the drive plate, use new self-locking bolts.

Engine removal and refitting

The engine can be parted from the gearbox or automatic transmission and removed alone from above, or it may be taken out, together with the gearbox or transmission, as an assembly, again lifting it upwards out of the engine compartment.

Normally it is best to hire a Renault lifting sling (Mot.477). It is also advisable to use a proper engine hoist.

If an improvised rope or wire sling must be used, make sure that this is sufficiently strong and check that it is fitted so that it cannot damage any auxiliaries.

Nylon-cord multiple-pulley hoists can be purchased from most accessory dealers and can handle the weight safely, but be sure that the beam to which the hoist is attached is strong enough. To provide a safety factor, it should be able to support the weight of at least three men at the centre. If a suitable beam is not available or if you are working in the open it will be necessary to buy or hire an engine lifting tripod or gantry or to make one from scaffold poles and clamps.

9.21 Removing the engine alone

Materials: Any spares found to be necessary, including new roll pins for universal joints and new engine mounting rubbers. See also sections in Chapters 10, 13 and 16 mentioned in text.

Tools: Spanners. Sockets. Pliers. Screwdrivers. Pin-punches. Lifting sling. Jack. Axle stands. Engine lifting hoist. Gantry or tripod, if required. See also sections in Chapters 10, 13 and 16 mentioned in text.

1 Preliminary work includes disconnecting the battery, raising the bonnet as high as possible and tying it back, draining the engine and gearbox oil and disconnecting the various hoses, wires and cables from the engine.

2 Drain the cooling system and remove the fan and pulley. Remove the radiator. (Chapter 10.)

3 Remove the air cleaner, take off the starter-motor heat shield, disconnect the starter-motor cables and remove the starter as described in Chapter 16.

4 When an automatic transmission is fitted, disconnect the governor operating cable, the vacuum capsule pipe and the transmission wiring harness – see Chapter 13.

5 On all engines take off the oil filter, remove the radiator and its shroud, the fan, water-pump pulley and crankshaft nose pulley. In the latter case, see Section 9.13.

6 Take off the cross-member between the side-members and the anti-roll bar to allow the exhaust pipe to drop as far as possible. Remove the engine dephaser (anti-vibration damper), front mountings, the clutch shield and the bolts which couple the engine to the gearbox.

7 When an automatic transmission is fitted, take out the top bolts which secure the transmission to the engine and the two fixing studs, using two nuts, locked one against the other, to unscrew them. Also take off the converter shield and unscrew the transmission bottom fixing bolts and the three bolts which secure the converter driving plate.

8 The lifting sling can now be attached and the weight of the engine taken with the block and tackle.

9 Next disconnect the exhaust pipe from the engine manifold and remove the bottom fixing nut on the right-hand engine mounting pad, and the three bolts which secure this pad to the cylinder block.

10 Repeat the operation on the left-hand side of the engine.

11 Raise the engine until the top of the gearbox touches the steering cross-member and place a jack

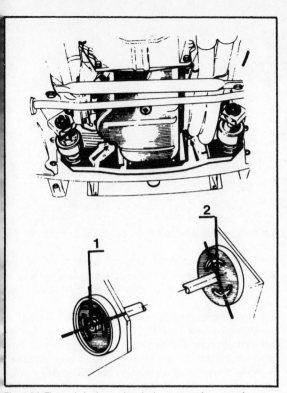

Fig. 9.24 The pads in the engine dephaser must be correctly lined-up as shown, with the centre-line of the front pad 1, at right-angles to the rear pad 2.

under the gearbox to keep it in this position while the right-hand bracket, mounting pad and side stiffener, plus the left-hand bracket, are removed.

12 Pull the engine forward and carefully manoeuvre it out of the engine compartment. It is particularly important, when a synchromesh gearbox is fitted, not to allow the weight of the engine to be carried by the clutch shaft (the gearbox input shaft) as this could bend the shaft or damage the clutch.

13 If an automatic transmission is fitted, bolt a strip of steel to one of the holes in the flange of the converter housing to prevent the converter dropping out of place.

14 Refitting the engine is a reversal of the removal sequence. When a synchromesh gearbox is fitted, lubricate the clutch-shaft splines lightly with molybdenum disulphide grease and be very careful not to allow the weight of the engine to be carried by the shaft as it is slid into place. Instructions for coupling-up the engine and transmission will be found in Chapter 13. On an automatic model it will be necessary to adjust the kick-down switch and the governor setting.

9.22 Removing and refitting the engine and the gearbox or transmission as an assembly

When the engine and the gearbox or automatic transmission are to be removed as an assembly, the operations will be the same as those described for removing the engine alone, but with the following exceptions –

1 The starter and the clutch shield need not be removed and the engine-mounting pads are left in place for removal later – see item 3.

2 It will be necessary to disconnect the drive shafts from the gearbox or transmission as described in Chapter 13 and also to disconnect the speedometer cable, the clutch cable and the gearshift link bolt when a synchromesh gearbox is fitted. On an automatic-transmission model the selector control mechanism must be disconnected as described in Chapter 13.

3 With both manual and automatic transmissions the gearbox cross-member must be taken off before the assembly can be lifted out. With the engine raised, the right-hand mounting pad and the left-hand bracket can be removed.

4 When refitting the engine and gearbox or transmission assembly, it will be necessary to couple-up the drive shafts as described in Chapter 13 and adjust the clutch operating clearance if a synchromesh gearbox is fitted, or the kick-down switch and governor control cable of an automatic transmission, as also described in Chapter 13.

10 The cooling system

A sealed, pressurized cooling system is used on all models. The coolant – a mixture of water, ethylene glycol and corrosion inhibitors – is drawn from the base of the radiator by a pump, circulated through the engine and returned to the top of the radiator. Smaller hoses feed coolant to the heater radiator when required and to the inlet manifold or the carburettor mounting flange to provide reasonably constant temperature for the carburettor and inlet passages.

The radiator has a simple filler plug and is kept full at all times. The coolant expands, of course, as it warms up and the surplus flows through an overflow pipe into an expansion bottle, fitted with a cap containing a valve which opens to relieve any excess pressure in the system.

As the engine cools down, fluid is drawn back through the overflow pipe to the radiator. At the same time the valve of the expansion bottle allows air to enter the bottle, preventing the creation of a semi-vacuum in the system.

The system normally requires no attention, other than checking the level in the expansion bottle, for about three years or until about 27 000 miles have been covered. By then, most of the corrosion inhibitor in the coolant will have become exhausted and it is necessary to drain the system, flush it out and refill it.

The time factor

Routine jobs such as topping up, draining and flushing the system, checking for leaks, and so on, do not call for preplanning. Suggested times for other jobs are: Removing and refitting the thermostat, 40 min; removing and refitting the radiator, 1 hr; fitting a new drive belt, 30 min; adjusting the belt tension, 10–20 min; fitting a new water pump, 1 hr.

10.1 Topping-up the system

The coolant level in the expansion bottle (on the right-hand side of the engine compartment) should be checked when the system is cold. It should be between the two marks which are moulded on the side of the bottle.

If the cap needs to be removed when the engine is hot, place a cloth over it and unscrew it slowly. *Allow all steam or air pressure to escape before removing the cap.*

If frequent topping-up is needed, check the system for leaks (see Section 10.2). Use the Renault coolant or the correct proportion of water and anti-freeze for topping up (one-third of anti-freeze for temperate climates) to prevent the risk of weakening the anti-freezing solution (see also Section 10.3). Renault dealers can check the specific gravity of the system with a special hydrometer, to ensure that there is an adequate safety margin. If plain water has to be used in an emergency, drain the system as soon as possible afterwards and refill it with the correct coolant.

If the cap is very tight, it may be necessary to use a strap wrench to unscrew it. If you have purchased a wrench to unscrew the oil filter this will probably be quite suitable. Obviously, force must be applied carefully owing to the risk of breaking the glass bottle.

Whenever the radiator filler cap or the expansion bottle is removed or refitted, the rubber seal must be renewed. If the old seal is refitted coolant leakage will occur and the system may overheat, as indicated by the oil pressure/water-temperature warning light on the instrument panel being illuminated.

To top-up the bottle –

1 Unscrew the cap from the top of the expansion bottle, which is fitted on the right-hand side of the engine compartment.

2 Top-up the fluid to bring the level between the two marks.

3 Refit the cap to the bottle, run the engine until it reaches its normal temperature and check for leaks.

10.2 Checking for leaks

It is often difficult to trace the source of a small leak which necessitates frequent topping-up. Perished water hoses are likely culprits. Get the engine really hot

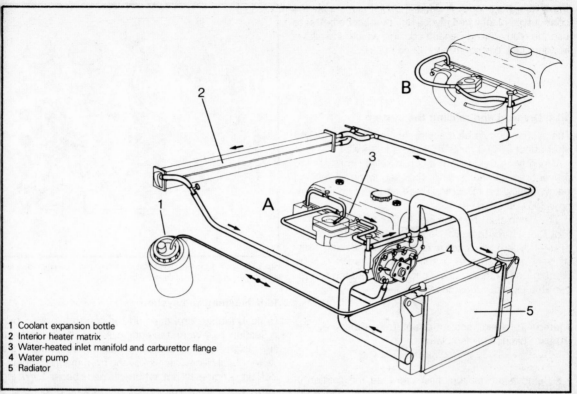

1 Coolant expansion bottle
2 Interior heater matrix
3 Water-heated inlet manifold and carburettor flange
4 Water pump
5 Radiator

Fig. 10.1 The components of the cooling system. The arrangement shown at A is that used with 1177 and 1337 models and that at B with 1170, 1171 and 1330 cars. The fan (not shown) is bolted to the flange of the water pump.

and rev it up while carefully examining each hose. It is a good plan to renew the hoses and the expansion bottle valve every three years.

If you are really baffled, a Renault dealer will be able to check the system by using a combined pump and pressure gauge which is connected in place of the radiator filler cap.

Sometimes internal seepage occurs past the cylinder-head gasket. Tighten the cylinder-head nuts progressively, *using a torque wrench, to the torque quoted in Chapter 17.* If necessary, ask a garage to do this for you.

A preparation known as Bars Leaks, obtainable from garages and accessory shops, will usually cure internal seepages and external leaks very effectively. It is an inexpensive precaution to add it to the cooling water whenever the system is flushed-out and refilled.

10.3 Anti-freeze solution.

When the car leaves the factory the anti-freeze mixture for use in temperate countries will provide protection against frost down to −30°C (−22°F). Vehicles exported to countries which experience very cold winters are protected down to −40°C (−40°F).

It is important to use a properly-inhibited anti-freeze to prevent any risk of corroding the aluminium cylinder head, or the aluminium radiator matrix which may be

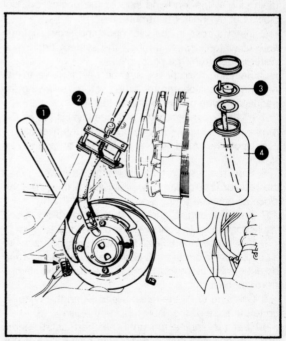

Fig. 10.2 Before removing the cap from the cooling system expansion bottle when the engine is hot, fit a clamp, 2, to the hose. A suitable tool, 1, can be used to free a tight cap. The expansion valve is shown at 3 and the bottle at 4. The spring shown by the arrow should not be fully compressed.

fitted to a later model. A Renault dealer can supply the correct type of inhibited glycol, but it would be better to use the ready-mixed Renault coolant, which is available in 2 litre (3½ pint) or 10 litre (2 gal) tins.

10.4 Draining and refilling the system

The system should be drained, flushed-out and refilled after about 27 000 miles or 3 years in service.

When filling the system it is particularly important to prevent any air-locks and the sequence described below should be followed. Three air-bleed screws are provided – see Fig. 10.3.

The clamp also shown in Fig. 10.3 is a Renault special tool, Mot.453, but a similar clamp can be made from strips of steel, drilled at the ends to take screws and nuts. Alternatively, a G-clamp or a self-locking wrench can be used, provided that suitable packing is inserted to prevent the pipe being damaged.

Materials: Renault coolant or anti-freeze mixture.
Tools: Spanners. Hose clamp.

1 Remove the radiator filler cap (see the caution in Section 10.1). Open the drain plug in the underside of the radiator bottom tank and open the tap or remove the drain plug in the left-hand side of the engine cylinder block. Set the heater control to 'Hot'.

2 Insert a hose in the filler neck and allow a gentle flow of water to pass through the system until clean water issues from the plug holes.

3 Refit the drain plugs, set the heater valve to the heating-on position and refill the system, following the sequence given below to prevent air-locks.

4 Fill the expansion bottle until the level is 1¼ in. (32 mm) above the upper level mark. Refit the filler cap.

5 Open the bleed screws 1, 2 and 3 shown in Fig. 10.3.

6 Refill the system through the radiator filler. When the radiator is full, clamp hoses 4 and 5 (Fig. 10.3) as close as possible to the water pump.

7 Start the engine and run it at a fast idling speed while continuing to pour water into the radiator filler.

8 When continuous jets of water, with no traces of air bubbles, run out of the bleed screws, close them *and do not disturb them from now on.* Remove the clamps from the hoses.

9 Continue to fill the radiator and when the water is up to the base of the filler, replace the filler cap.

10 Let the engine run until the thermostat opens, which is indicated by the noticeable heating-up of the return hose to the radiator. Allow the engine to cool down and check that the level in the expansion bottle is correct.

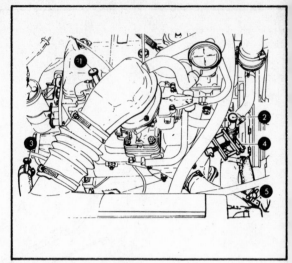

Fig. 10.3 Cooling system bleed screws, which must be opened when refilling the system, as described in the text.

10.5 Flushing the system

To flush the system, drain off the coolant as described in Section 10.4 when the engine is cold, insert a hose in the radiator filler and allow water to run through the system until clear water is flowing from the drain holes.

If the engine is hot when drained, *begin by using warm water to avoid any risk of cracking or distorting the cylinder head or block.*

After a fairly high mileage has been covered, normal flushing may not dislodge the sediment in the radiator, which must then be reverse-flushed by removing it, inverting it and connecting a hose to the outlet pipe so that a good flow of water under pressure can be forced through the matrix in the reverse direction to the normal flow. *Do not use a scale-removing compound before flushing.* It may corrode the aluminium components.

10.6 Renewing the expansion bottle valve

The valve at the top of the expansion bottle should not normally require servicing but if coolant should accidentally enter it at any time, it must be renewed. It is intended to pass only air.

If water is being lost and the hoses seem to be sound, have the valve checked by a Renault dealer. To do this he will connect a special test rig, consisting of a pressure gauge mounted on a hand pump, to an adaptor which screws into the radiator filler cap opening. The pressure in the system is pumped up to 0.9 bar (about 13 lb/sq in.) and then allowed to drop until it stabilizes at a reading on the gauge which should correspond with the presssure stamped on the valve, with a tolerance of 0.1 bar (about 2 lb per sq in.) each way.

This pressure is expressed in millibars. If the valve is set to open at 800 millibars, for example, this is equivalent to 0.8 on the gauge.

As the expansion tank valve plays an important part in

ensuring that the cooling system operates at its most efficient temperature, it is a good plan to change the valve as a precaution after two years in use, as described below –

Materials: New valve and gasket.
Tools: Strap-wrench, if cap is tight. Hose clamps – see Section 10.4.

1 Clamp the hose leading from the radiator to the valve.

2 Unscrew the valve cap, remove the valve and fit the replacement, with a new gasket *between the valve and the bottle*.

3 Screw the cap down firmly and remove the hose clamp.

4 Fill the bottle up to the upper level mark.

5 If the bottle has been removed, when refitting it tighten the clamping bolt that retains one end of the clamp until the spring coils touch and then unscrew it by one turn.

10.7 Checking the thermostat

The thermostat regulates the cooling-water temperature. It therefore has a vital effect on the engine efficiency and the fuel consumption. Thermostats, of course, are not infallible and if overheating occurs, or if the engine is slow to warm-up, it is logical to check this item; but remember that overheating can be caused by a number of other faults (see the chart in Chapter 5).

Many authorities recommend that the thermostat should be changed every two years, as corrosion, deposits of sludge or hard scale, or a distorted valve, can all cause sluggish action.

The thermostat is inserted in the outlet pipe of the pump housing. To remove and check it –

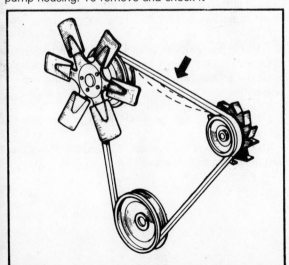

Fig. 10.4 When adjusting the fan belt it should be possible to deflect the centre of the run shown by the arrow by approximately ¼ in. (6.5-7.5 mm).

Materials: New thermostat, if required.
Tools: Screwdriver. Pliers. Pan of hot water. Thermometer (not essential).

1 Before disconnecting the hose and removing the thermostat, drain sufficient coolant to reduce the level to below the water pump. As you lift out the thermostat, note the position in which it was fitted in the housing.

2 When the thermostat is cold or warm, the valve should be closed. If it is open, discard the thermostat and fit a new one. If the valve is closed, suspend the thermostat in a pan of water which is nearly at boiling point. The valve should then open fully. If a suitable thermometer is available, the water can be heated while watching the operation of the thermostat. It should begin to open, and should be fully open, at the temperatures given in Chapter 17. Provided that a used thermostat is operating approximately within the range quoted it can be refitted.

3 When installing the thermostat, make sure that it is fitted correctly so that the water aperture is not blocked.

10.8 Adjusting the tension of the fan, water pump and generator driving belt

The correct tension of the driving belt is important. If the belt is too slack, it will slip, overheat, become glazed and will have a short life. Too tight a belt, on the other hand, will also have a short life and will place a heavy load on the bearings of the units which the belt drives.

Because of the importance of the correct tension, Renault dealers use a special tool to measure it, consisting of a bar which has at its centre a sliding plunger calibrated in millimetres. When checking at home, depress the belt at the centre of the run between the alternator and the fan pulleys, using firm thumb pressure. The belt should deflect about ¼ in. (6.5-7.5 mm) at the centre of its longest run, but when first fitted a new belt should deflect by about ³/₁₆ in. (4.5-5.5 mm) until it has been in use for about 300 miles.

Tools: Spanners.

1 The belt can be adjusted in the conventional manner by slackening the bolt in the slotted strut above the alternator and the pivot bolt, and swinging the generator towards or away from the engine.

2 If a lever is used to move the generator, *apply it only at the pulley end*.

10.9 Removing and refitting the water pump

The water pump is not designed to be serviced or overhauled. If it develops a leak past the spindle or its efficiency deteriorates – usually owing to corrosion of the impeller – the only cure is to fit a new pump cover or a complete pump.

If a replacement cover can be obtained, this will probably be sufficient since it contains the spindle, hub, bearings, impeller and the sealing rings. The pump body is simply a casting to which the hoses are connected and which houses the thermostat.

To change the pump cover alone –

Materials: New cover – and new hoses – if required. Gasket. Coolant.

Tools: Spanners. Soft-faced mallet. Screwdriver. Pliers.

1 Disconnect the battery, slacken the pump driving belt, remove the fan shroud, if fitted, and take off the fan, the water pump pulley and the driving belt.

2 Drain the cooling system to below the level of the pump and unscrew the nine bolts which retain the cover.

3 When refitting the cover, or a new cover, clean the gasket joint faces and fit the new gasket dry, without jointing compound.

4 Adjust the driving belt tension as described in Section 10.8, refill the cooling system and bleed it as described in Section 10.4.

To change the complete pump –

1 Carry out the preliminary draining and dismantling as described above and also remove the radiator.

2 Disconnect the hoses from the pump and remove the thermostat.

3 Take out the six bolts which retain the pump assembly (see Fig. 10.5) and free the pump from the cylinder head, tapping it if necessary with a soft-faced mallet to break the joint.

4 Before refitting the pump clean the gasket joint faces. Fit a new gasket, without jointing compound, and tighten the retaining bolts progressively to avoid distort-

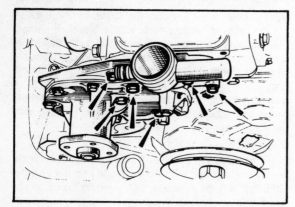

Fig. 10.5 The water pump assembly is retained by the bolts shown by the arrows. The other bolts retain only the pump cover.

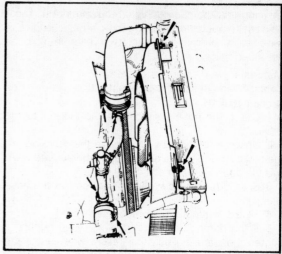

Fig. 10.6 When removing the radiator, the retaining nuts and hose clamping screws shown by the arrows must be undone.

ing the pump. After reconnecting the hoses, fill the cooling system and bleed it as described in Section 10.4, and tension the driving belt as described in Section 10.8.

10.10 Removing and refitting the radiator

A leak-stopping compound may be successful in curing a minor leak from the radiator, but persisting leakage or damage to the radiator calls for repair by a radiator specialist – especially when an aluminium matrix is fitted. As an alternative to having the existing radiator repaired, it may be cheaper to fit a reconditioned component.

To remove and refit the radiator –

Materials: New radiator hoses. Mounting rubbers. Coolant (if the old coolant is not to be re-used).

Tools: Spanners or sockets. Hose clamps – see Section 10.4.

1 Clamp the hoses down to the radiator and drain the radiator, or drain the complete system if fresh coolant is to be used. Disconnect the pipe leading to the expansion bottle.

2 Remove the fan shroud if necessary.

3 Remove the two bolts which retain the radiator. Lift out the radiator.

4 After refitting the radiator refill and bleed the system as described in Section 10.4.

11 The carburettor and petrol pump

As will be seen from the specifications in Chapter 17, Renault 12 models may be fitted with Solex or Weber carburettors. Solex carburettors are single-barrel types while Webers have twin barrels, each with its own choke, throttle and jet system, fed from a common float chamber.

When ordering spare parts such as jets or gaskets, it is important to quote the type and specification numbers which are stamped on a tag fitted under one of the float-chamber cover screws on a Solex carburettor, or on the base flange of a Weber.

The whole of the information must be quoted – such as Weber 32DIR–21–2302 – in order to ensure that the correct replacements are supplied.

It does sometimes happen, however, that the tag from a Solex carburettor is lost during dismantling and in such a case your dealer should be able to tell you the correct carburettor specification if you give him the vehicle type number and chassis number, and the engine type, model and number, taken from the data plates in the engine compartment.

The usual adjustments are provided on all carburettors for the idling speed and mixture strength. Other adjustments (depending on the model), which are normally needed only when the carburettor is being assembled, such as the float setting, fast-idle speed, initial throttle opening, acceleration pump stroke, and the de-fuming control valve, can be adjusted, but special gauges and setting tools must be used.

These adjustments, therefore, should never be disturbed in service. The work is definitely a job for a Renault dealer. It must also be remembered that these adjustments – and the jet settings – are critical in maintaining the acceptable legal standard of exhaust emissions.

The time factor

It is difficult to allot definite times to many carburettor jobs, especially when adjustment and tuning are involved. If you are a perfectionist, for example, it is quite possible to spend a morning or an afternoon on carburettor servicing and road-testing. Some suggested times are: Remove and refit the carburettor, 30 min; service the carburettor, 1 hr; carburettor idling adjustments, 45–60 min; clean or change the air cleaner element, 30 min; clean the fuel pump filter, 15 min; remove and refit the fuel pump, 30–40 min.

Carburettor idling adjustments

All engines are very sensitive to correct adjustment of the idling speed and mixture strength. If an engine will not tick-over properly, or stalls in traffic or when the throttle is suddenly closed, the most likely cause is incorrect setting of the idling speed and mixture control screws.

You cannot expect to obtain good idling, of course, if the air cleaner is dirty or if there are ignition or mechanical faults, but provided that an engine is otherwise in good tune, setting the idling adjustments is a straightforward job.

Don't try to obtain too slow a tick-over. The idling speed should be about 600–700 rpm, or slightly higher when an automatic transmission is fitted and the selector is at N or P. If the carburettor is adjusted to idle slowly when the engine is hot, stalling may be experienced when it is cold. Check by depressing the clutch pedal, or by selecting A when an automatic transmission is fitted. The idling speed should not drop excessively and the engine should not become 'lumpy'. *Do not rev the engine with A selected.* Even with the handbrake hard on the car may move forward.

11.1 To adjust all types of carburettors

Tools: A flexible-stem screwdriver, obtainable from Renault dealers (part No. Mot.561) makes it easier to reach the adjusting screws, but if this is not available the adjustments can be carried out with the air filter removed.

1 Adjust the air screw or the throttle-stop screw (Fig 11.1) to give an idling speed of about 700 rpm.

2 Turn the mixture screw in either direction until the highest possible idling speed is obtained and then readjust the speed with the air screw.

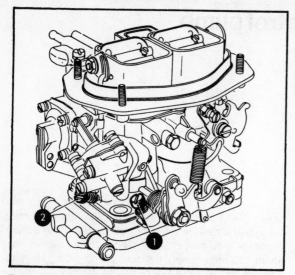

Fig. 11.1 The slow-running adjustments on a Weber carburettor. 1, idling speed adjustment. 2, mixture strength adjustment.

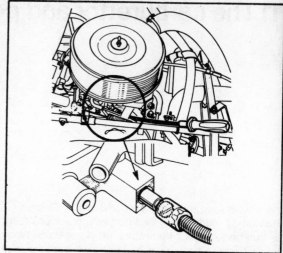

Fig. 11.3 A flexible screwdriver, obtainable from Renault dealers, simplifies carburettor adjustments.

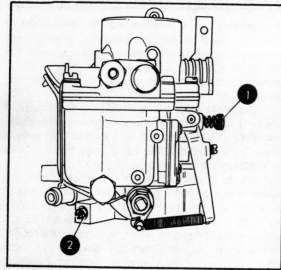

Fig. 11.2 Idling adjustments on a Solex carburettor. 1, idling speed adjustment. 2, mixture strength adjustment.

3 Repeat the adjustments once or twice to make sure that the mixture screw is giving the highest idling speed and then readjust the air screw to restore the correct idling speed.

4 When the settings have been stabilized in this way, finally screw in the mixture screw so that the engine speed drops slightly (by about 25 rpm if a rev counter is fitted) to reduce the exhaust pollution to an acceptable figure.

11.2 Cleaning the float chamber and jets

It should not be necessary to carry out a routine check of the carburettor, including cleaning the float chamber, jets and jet passages, at very frequent intervals, but it is worth doing this during the 12 000-mile service in order

to forestall possible trouble. A certain amount of very fine sediment finds its way past the filters and this, together with globules of water, will accumulate in the float-chamber bowl, causing misfiring, poor idling or difficult starting, depending on which jets have become clogged.

For routine servicing it is not necessary to remove the carburettor from the engine but before dismantling it, thoroughly clean the outside, so that there is no risk of transferring dirt and grit into the vulnerable interior passage.

Materials: Any new parts required. New gaskets and sealing washers.

Tools: Screwdriver. Pointed-nose pliers. Small spanners.

1 Remove the air-cleaner.

2 Disconnect the choke link rod when necessary *but be careful not to alter any adjustments.*

3 Remove the upper part of the carburettor body, taking care that the gasket is not torn. If there is any doubt about its condition, fit a new gasket.

4 Remove the float and the needle valve. Check for

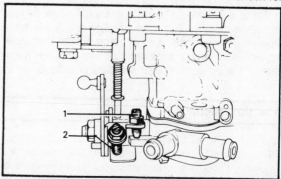

Fig. 11.4 The stop-screw 1, and the initial throttle opening screw 2 of a Solex EISA-4 carburettor must not be disturbed.

leakage of petrol into the float. Unscrew the needle valve body from the carburettor and swill it in petrol. Make sure that the tip of the valve is not ridged and that the valve slides freely in the body. If there is any doubt about the valve, fit a new assembly.

5 If a filter is fitted in the carburettor fuel inlet on Solex carburettors it is retained by the inlet union. On Weber carburettors unscrew the plug from the underside of the upper body, beneath the fuel inlet, and remove the gauze filter. Swill the filter in petrol and make sure that the mesh is not damaged.

6 Wash out the float chamber with petrol, being careful to remove any sediment.

7 Remove the jets. These are clearly shown in the illustrations.

8 Wash the jets in petrol, blow through them in the reverse direction to the normal petrol flow to make sure that the drillings are clear and flush-out the jet passages with petrol. *Do not probe the jets with wire* — this will damage the carefully calibrated drillings and upset engine performance.

Special notes

Do not dismantle the carburettor further than just described. The linkage that controls the action of the two throttles of a twin-barrel carburettor, the accelerator pump stroke and the fast-idling speed of both types when the choke is in use, must be accurately adjusted. As was emphasized earlier, this is definitely a job for a Renault dealer or a carburettor specialist. If the adjustments have not been tampered with, they cannot alter of their own accord.

When hot-water hoses are connected to the carburettor flange, clamp the hoses as close as possible to the carburettor before disconnecting them, if the carburettor is to be removed for servicing. This will avoid the necessity for bleeding and topping-up the system as described in Chapter 10 when the carburettor has been refitted.

The carburettor air filter

If the filter element is allowed to become clogged, performance will suffer and fuel consumption will be increased, owing to the restriction on the air entering the carburettor. The filter should be serviced at 12 000-mile intervals or more frequently in dusty conditions.

On some engines an adjustable flap allows warm air to be drawn from near the exhaust manifold in cold weather. This improves the engine flexibility and the fuel consumption in cold weather and helps to prevent the carburettor icing-up. The lever should be in the upper position when the temperature is below about 5–10°C (40–50°F) and should be moved towards the carburettor during the summer months. On some models the flap is thermostatically controlled. If this should fail, have a word with your Renault dealer.

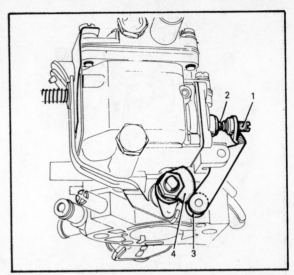

Fig. 11.5 The accelerator pump linkage on a Solex EISA-4 carburettor. The adjusting screw 1, which acts on the pump plunger 2, must not be altered. The cam 4 operates the pump lever through the roller 3.

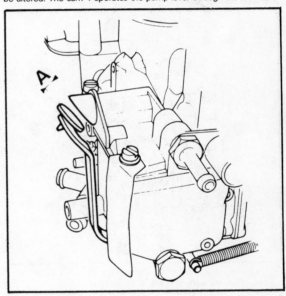

Fig. 11.6 Another adjustment on the Solex EISA-4 which should not be altered unnecessarily. The de-fuming valve opening A is pre-set and should be 3-4 mm (1/8-5/32 in.).

11.3 Changing the carburettor air filter

1 Remove the end cover from the air cleaner.

2 Slide out the element. Tap it to remove dust, or renew it if it is badly choked or greasy. *Do not* wash it in petrol.

3 When refitting the top cover, do not overtighten the retaining nuts.

The petrol pump

Provided that the filter is cleaned at regular intervals as

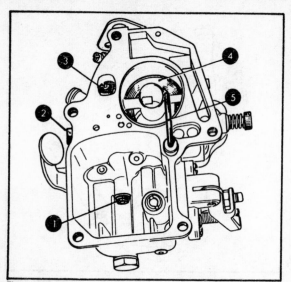

Fig. 11.7 The jets of a Solex 32 EISA carburettor. 1, main jet. 2, idling jet. 3, air compensator jet. 4, choke tube. 5, accelerator pump discharge tube and jet.

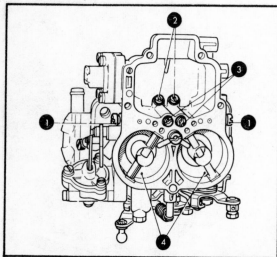

Fig. 11.8 The jets of a Weber dual-barrel carburettor. 1, idling jet. 2, main jets. 3, air-compensating jets. 4, choke tubes.

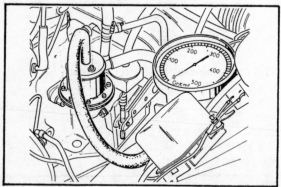

Fig. 11.9 A Renault dealer can use a special gauge to check the pressure developed by the fuel pump. One of the filter cover screws is shown at 1. The flange nuts 2 should be kept tight.

described below, the mechanically-operated petrol pump should seldom give trouble.

If the pump does not deliver petrol to the carburettor, make sure there is fuel in the tank (the petrol gauge may be faulty) and check that the unions in the pipe connecting the tank to the pump are tight. Also see that the pump filter is clean, that the gasket is in good condition, and that the clamping screw is firmly tightened. An air leak at the gasket is the most frequent cause of pump failure.

If, after extended service, an early type of pump begins to give trouble, it is not advisable to attempt to repair it without special equipment. The most satisfactory course is to take advantage of the service-exchange scheme operated by Renault dealers, under which a reconditioned pump can be fitted at quite a modest cost. The later type of pump cannot be repaired.

A Renault dealer will be able to test the pressure developed by the pump and the rate of fuel flow, with the aid of a special test kit; and this is most important, as too low a pressure can cause fuel starvation at high speeds, and possibly serious damage to the valves and pistons, while too high a pressure is likely to result in excessive petrol consumption and carburettor flooding.

11.4 Cleaning the petrol pump filter

Tools: Spanner. Old toothbrush or paintbrush. Clean cloth.

1 Disconnect the tank-to-pump fuel feed pipe at the union on the pump and clamp or plug the end of the pipe to prevent fuel draining from the tank.

2 Unscrew the setscrews that retain the filter cover and remove the cover.

3 Remove the filter and clean it with petrol, using an old toothbrush or a paintbrush and taking care not to damage the mesh. Mop out any sediment which has accumulated in the base of the filter chamber.

4 Make sure that the gasket beneath the filter cover is in good condition. An air leak here can put the pump out of action.

5 Check the tightness of the bolts that retain the pump on the crankcase and the condition of the fuel hoses and clips.

Emission-control equipment

Special exhaust-gas emission carburettors are fitted to models exported to some countries (the USA, for example) where strict emission regulations must be complied with.

Servicing and adjusting this equipment must be left to a Renault dealer, as special instruments are needed to check that the exhaust emissions are within the legal limits. This also applies to the fuel-vapour recuperation equipment that prevents the escape of petrol fumes into the atmosphere.

12 The ignition system

Given conscientious maintenance, there is no reason why the ignition system should prove troublesome — yet it shares with the carburettor the doubtful distinction of being responsible for a large percentage of roadside breakdowns, starting problems, loss of power and heavy fuel consumption.

Most of these faults can usually be blamed on inefficient servicing and when an emission-control carburettor is fitted, incorrect ignition timing can also cause persistent trouble with engine flat-spots and stalling. Where strict emission regulations are in force the wrong settings may put the car outside the legal limits for exhaust-gas pollution.

When we recommend that some of the checks and adjustments on later cars should be done by a Renault dealer, therefore, we have all these considerations very much in mind. Fortunately, the average owner should be able to carry out most of the work described in this chapter.

The time factor

None of the jobs described in the following sections is very time-consuming. For example: Cleaning and gapping the sparking plugs, 30 min; cleaning and lubricating the distributor, 25 min; removing the distributor contacts, refitting and adjusting the gap, 40–50 min; removing and refitting the distributor, 30 min; checking and adjusting the ignition timing, 20 min.

12.1 Cleaning and adjusting the sparking plugs

The correct type of plug is given in Chapter 17. Plugs which have similar characteristics are available from other sparking-plug manufacturers, *but it is essential to make sure that the correct 'heat' grade is used.* Fit new plugs after 10 000 miles in service — it will pay dividends in better performance and improved fuel consumption.

The use of a garage plug-cleaner is the only really effective method of removing carbon and other deposits from the internal surfaces and insulators of the plugs.

When removing and refitting the plugs be careful not to cross-thread them. Repairing damaged threads in an aluminium cylinder head can be expensive, although a Renault dealer or an engineering shop should be able to salvage the head by fitting a special thread insert.

To avoid the risk of accidental 'shorts', disconnect the battery before starting work.

Bearing these points in mind, remove and clean the plugs as follows —

Tools: Sparking-plug spanner. Wire brush. Gap gauge and file.

1 Pull of the connectors — don't pull on the wires themselves — and unscrew the plugs. Keep the spanner square to avoid cracking the external insulators. Neglected plugs can be very tight.

2 Clean the points with a wire brush. If the internal insulators are dirty, or the plugs have been in service for more than 6000 miles (10 000 km) have them cleaned by a garage.

3 Open the gap by bending the *side* electrode only and file the sparking surfaces square to each other with clean, sharp edges. This will reduce the voltage needed to produce a good spark.

4 Set the gap between the points to 0.025 in. (0.6 mm), using an inexpensive gauge and setting tool such as the Champion plug-servicing tool sold by accessory shops, which also includes an electrode file. Bend the *side* electrode only.

5 Clean the threaded portion of each plug with a stiff brush and smear a trace of graphite grease on the threads.

6 Blow or wipe any dust or grit out of the plug recesses in the cylinder head. Make sure that the sealing washers are in good condition and seated properly on the plugs, and screw the plugs home by turning the plug spanner *without using the tommy-bar.*

Use the tommy bar only for the final half-turn to ensure a gas-tight joint. Over-tightening is unnecessary and is likely to lead to trouble. If the plugs cannot be screwed in easily by hand, ask your garage to clean-up the threads in the cylinder head with a plug-thread tap.

12.2 The ignition coil and high-tension leads

The coil requires little or no attention, apart from keeping it clean — particularly the moulded cap — and making sure that the connections are clean and tight. An internal fault in the coil will show up on an electronic test set.

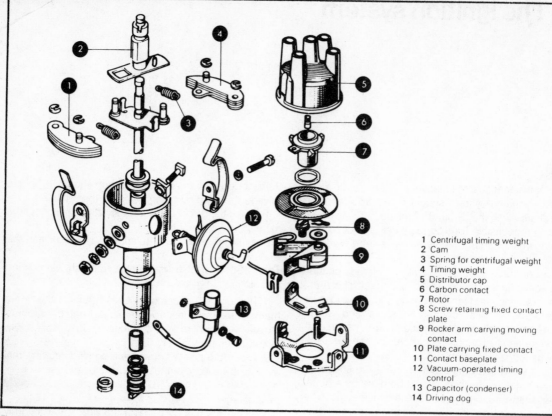

1 Centrifugal timing weight
2 Cam
3 Spring for centrifugal weight
4 Timing weight
5 Distributor cap
6 Carbon contact
7 Rotor
8 Screw retaining fixed contact
   plate
9 Rocker arm carrying moving
   contact
10 Plate carrying fixed contact
11 Contact baseplate
12 Vacuum-operated timing
   control
13 Capacitor (condenser)
14 Driving dog

Fig. 12.1 A typical ignition distributor fully dismantled.

Otherwise, the only practicable test is to substitute, temporarily, a coil that is known to be in good condition.

Test the high-tension leads between the coil and the distributor and between the distributor cap and the sparking plugs for surface cracks by doubling the cables between the fingers. Renew them if necessary. The modern resistance type of lead should be changed, as a precaution, after two years. Never try to fit new terminals to the leads. A complete pre-assembled set must be used.

12.3 The ignition capacitor

An inefficient capacitor or condenser will cause rapid burning of the contact-breaker points and a weak spark or – if it should short-circuit internally – failure of the plugs to fire at all. The capacitor is attached to the side of the distributor.

Test by substituting a new capacitor for the doubtful one, but first check for a break or short-circuit in the flexible lead that connects it to the contact-breaker terminal post – a cause of misfiring or complete cutting-out of the ignition that is often overlooked. As an insurance against future trouble, fit a new capacitor whenever the contact-breaker points are renewed. It is not an expensive item.

12.4 Lubricating the ignition distributor

Over-lubrication should be avoided. If grease or oil is thrown on to the contact points, it will be carbonized and cause misfiring.

Materials: Engine oil. Grease.

1 Remove the distributor cap and pull the rotor off the end of the shaft. Remove the circular plate (when fitted), exposing the contact-breaker mechanism.

2 Apply two drops of engine oil to the lubricating pad in the top of the distributor shaft and smear just a trace of grease on the lobes of the cam.

3 Drip a few drops of oil through the hole in the contact-breaker baseplate, to lubricate the centrifugal advance mechanism.

4 Replace the plate. Push the rotor on to the end of the shaft, making sure that the driving lug engages with the slot in the shaft and that the rotor is pushed down as far as possible.

12.5 Cleaning the distributor cap and rotor

1 Lightly scrape the contact strip on the rotor and the terminals inside the cap to expose bright metal. *Do not file them or rub them down with emery paper.*

2 Check the carbon contact inside the distributor cap. Do not over-stretch the spring.

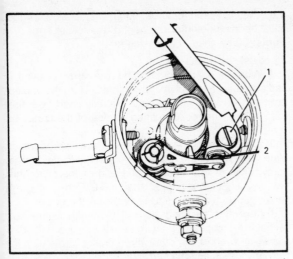

Fig. 12.2 Adjusting the contact-breaker points. Slacken the screw 1 and use a screwdriver to move the contact plate to give the correct gap at 2.

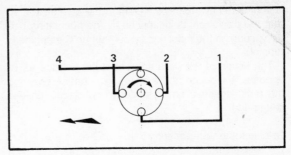

Fig. 12.4 The sparking plug leads must be connected to the distributor cap in the order shown. The arrow indicates the front of the car, No. 1 plug being at the *rear* of the engine.

3 Examine the rotor for signs of 'tracking' in the form of dark tracks on the surface of the plastic. If this has occurred, or if the tip of the terminal is badly burnt, fit a new rotor.

4 Wipe the interior of the cap with a cloth moistened with methylated spirits (denatured alcohol) to remove dust or oily deposits, which will provide a leakage path for the high-tension current. A cracked cap or condensed moisture on the inside or outside of the cap is a common cause of difficult starting and misfiring. An occasional spray with a water-repelling aerosol will cure and prevent condensation troubles.

12.6 Testing the distributor cap and rotor

1 Detach two alternative sparking-plug leads, and the distributor-end of the coil high-tension lead, from the cap. Insert the end of the coil lead into each of the empty sockets in turn. Leave the remaining leads in place and connected to sparking plugs.

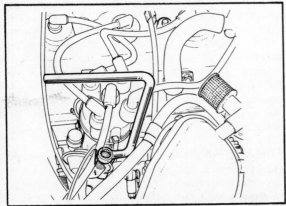

Fig. 12.3 This special cranked spanner is useful when slackening and tightening the distributor clamping bolt.

2 Switch on the ignition, make sure that the contact-breaker points are closed, and with the tip of a screwdriver flick the points apart. If there has been any tracking, a spark will jump across the interior of the distributor cap.

The rotor can be checked for breakdown of the insulation as follows, without removing it from the cam spindle —

1 Remove the coil high-tension lead from the distributor cap.

2 Hold the end almost in contact with the edge of the rotor blade and flick the contact-breaker points open as before. If the rotor is faulty a spark will jump the air gap between the high-tension lead and the rotor blade. Occasionally, internal leakage develops from the underside of the electrode of the rotor, through the plastic to the interior surface, allowing the high-tension current to jump to the cam spindle and so to earth. This can be a very elusive fault to spot but will be revealed by the above test. Fit a new rotor whenever you fit new sparking plugs and you should have no trouble.

12.7 Checking the automatic timing controls

The timing of the spark varies under running conditions. It must occur earlier as the engine speed increases but must be retarded, to prevent detonation or 'pinking', when the engine is under load.

A centrifugal control which responds to engine speed, takes the form of two small weights below the contact-breaker baseplate in the distributor. Provided that it receives regular lubrication, the centrifugal timing control seldom gives trouble.

If a spring should break, it is essential to renew both springs, making sure that they are of the correct part number for the engine. Their strength determines the shape of the advance curve, giving the correct amount of advance for any speed. As recommended in Section 12.11, renewal of the springs and checking the advance curve must be left to a Renault dealer.

A vacuum-operated control is fitted to some distributors in addition to the centrifugal control. The circular housing seen in Fig. 12.1 contains a diaphragm and is connected by a pipe to a point in the carburettor, so that the diaphragm is influenced by the fluctuating partial vacuum in the induction system when the engine is running.

The action of the vacuum control either adds to, or opposes, the action of the centrifugal control, ensuring the most effective timing under all conditions of load and speed.

To check the vacuum control –

1 Make sure that the suction chamber does not contain any condensed fuel. Test the action of the diaphragm by applying suction to the union. If the diaphragm appears to be faulty, fit a new unit.

2 Check the rubber connections at each end of the vacuum pipe and renew them if they have split or are a loose fit on the pipe. Even a slight air leak will affect the action of the control.

12.8 Checking, removing and refitting the contact-breaker points

It is not necessary to remove the distributor from the engine in order to check the points.

Materials: Replacement contact-breaker set. Clean cloth. Petrol. Engine oil. Grease.
Tools: Screwdriver. Pliers.

To inspect or renew the points –

1 Remove the distributor cap by springing the clips aside and pull off the rotor arm. Gentle leverage may be used if the rotor is tight. Remove the circular plate, when fitted.

2 Lever the pivoted contact away from the fixed one. The points should have a clean, frosted appearance.

3 If the contacts are blackened, dirty or pitted, renew them. Slacken the nut on the terminal on the side of the distributor to free the fixed end of the contact-breaker spring (which is slotted to allow it to be disengaged easily), pull off the spring clip that retains the contact-breaker arm and remove the arm.

4 Remove the screw that retains the fixed contact plate and take out the plate.

5 Before fitting a new contact set, clean the contact points with petrol. Lubricate the cam with a light smear of grease.

6 Adjust the contact-breaker gap as described in Section 12.9 and check the ignition timing as described in Section 12.12.

12.9 Adjusting the contact-breaker gap

The contact-breaker gap should not be measured with a feeler gauge unless the contact faces have been trued-up to remove the pip and crater, or a new set of contacts has been installed.

When new contacts have been fitted, check the gap

after they have run for about 500 miles, to allow for the initial bedding-down of the heel of the rocker arm.
Tools: Screwdriver. Feeler gauge.

To adjust the points –

1 With the distributor cap and rotor arm removed – and also the circular plate, when fitted – turn the engine until the contact-breaker points are fully open, with the fibre heel of the rocker resting on one of the crests of the cam.

2 Slacken the screw that retains the fixed contact plate and move the plate by inserting the tip of a screwdriver in the notch at one end of the plate and twisting it. Set the gap so that a 0.016 in. (0.4 mm) feeler gauge is a light drag fit between the points.

3 After the securing screw has been tightened, recheck the gap and then measure the gap with the rocker on each of the other three crests of the cam in turn. If there is any marked difference in the gaps, the cam or the spindle bearing, or both, are worn. If the bearing is worn a new distributor body will be required and it would be better to fit a new distributor – see Section 12.11.

4 Check the ignition timing as described in Section 12.12. Any alteration of the contact-breaker gap will alter the timing.

12.10 Removing and refitting the distributor

Tools: Spanners or Ele.556 (special cranked spanner).

1 Remove the distributor cap.

2 Disconnect the vacuum advance pipe from the distributor.

3 Disconnect the low-tension lead from the terminal on the side of the distributor.

4 Remove the nut securing the clamp plate and remove the distributor.

5 When refitting the distributor refer to Section 12.12.

12.11 Dismantling and reassembling the distributor

Whenever a distributor is stripped and rebuilt, it must be checked to make sure that the vacuum-operated automatic advance control, when fitted, and also the centrifugal control, are operating correctly. This is particularly important in the case of emission-controlled engines.

With a Ducellier distributor, if the adjustment of the toothed segment to which the vacuum timing control is attached is disturbed, the timing of the engine under running conditions will be upset and the segment will have to be readjusted by a Renault dealer, using special test equipment.

The action of the various controls can be checked only by using a distributor test-bench, which means either that the checks will have to be done by a dealer or by an auto-electrician. It may be more economical, therefore, to fit a service-exchange distributor, and this must be done if the shaft and bushes are worn.

12.12 Checking and adjusting the ignition timing

We have already emphasized the importance of correct ignition timing, especially when an emission-control carburettor is fitted.

The distributor shaft is driven by an offset dog at its lower end which engages with the driving dog at the top of a shaft in the cylinder block, driven by a skew gear from the camshaft. The basic timing cannot be lost, therefore, unless the engine has been dismantled or the shaft in the cylinder block has been removed for some other reason (see Chapter 9).

To refit the distributor, slide it into position with the vacuum-advance unit facing outwards, away from the cylinder block, turn the rotor until the drive is felt to engage, and push it fully home.

Fit the clamp or the locking bolt and tighten the nut or the bolt just sufficiently to allow the distributor to be rotated by hand in order to adjust the timing.

The correct timing is then obtained by rotating the distributor body through a few degrees in either direction. The timing marks are clearly shown in Figs. 5 and 12.6 and the correct settings for the various engines are listed in Chapter 17.

Methods of turning the engine are described on page 16.

To set the static timing (ie, when the engine is not running) –

Tools: Spanners, including sparking-plug spanner. Test lamp and leads (optional). Torch or inspection lamp if required.

1 Remove the sparking plugs and the valve cover and turn the engine until the piston in No. 1 cylinder (at the *rear* of the engine) is at the top of the compression stroke, when both valves will be closed. Line-up the timing marks correctly.

2 Remove the distributor cap and make sure that the centrifugal advance weights are not binding by turning the rotor clockwise and releasing it. Check that the contact-breaker baseplate is free to rotate slightly.

3 Slacken the distributor clamping nut if this has not been done previously. The nut is not too accessible on some models and Renault dealers have a cranked spanner, Ele.556, which is very useful when making timing adjustments.

4 Set the timing by rotating the distributor body clockwise until the contact points are just closed and then slowly turn it anti-clockwise until they just separate. If the ignition is switched on, a small spark can be seen and heard to jump across the points as they separate.

5 A more accurate method of checking the opening of the points is to connect a side-lamp bulb, mounted in a suitable holder, between the low-tension terminal on the side of the distributor body and a clean unpainted metal part of the engine. When the points are closed, with the ignition switched on, the lamp will not be

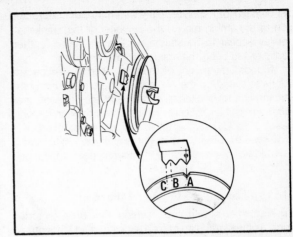

Fig. 12.5 When the timing indicator is on the crankshaft pulley, the top-dead-centre position is reached when the notch A is opposite the pointer which has a hole drilled in it. When the notch is 7 mm to the left of the first pointer, approximately at B, the timing is 6° btdc; and when it is opposite the first pointer, at C, the timing is 10° btdc with a manual transmission or 12° btdc with an automatic transmission.

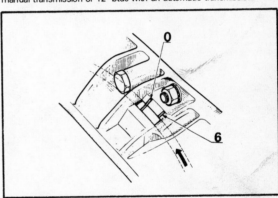

Fig. 12.6 An alternative type of timing indicator takes the form of a line on the flywheel which is aligned with notches on the flywheel housing. The 'O' mark shown represents the top-dead-centre and the '6' mark 6° btdc.

alight. At the instant that they open, it will light-up. When checking the opening point, keep a light finger pressure on the rotor in an anti-clockwise direction to take up backlash in the drive. Tighten the clamping bolt and recheck the timing.

6 If it is necessary to turn the distributor through a considerable angle from the initial position in which it was fitted, the gears are not meshing correctly, being one or more teeth out. Withdraw the distributor shaft and refit it correctly as described in Chapter 9, Section 9.18. When the right timing has been obtained, tighten the clamping nut or screw to prevent the distributor body from rotating and then recheck the timing.

12.13 Timing with a stroboscopic lamp

Renault recommend that the timing should be set with the engine idling and the vacuum advance pipe disconnected, using a stroboscopic timing lamp which is connected to No. 1 sparking plug. When the light is directed on to the timing marks, the flywheel or the crankshaft pulley appear to be stationary. The distributor is then adjusted to bring the marks into alignment.

A good timing light of the type used in service stations to speed-up the job of checking and adjusting the timing is a fairly expensive item and the cheaper ones that are sold by accessory shops have their limitations. Careful setting of the static timing as just described, followed by a road test as outlined in the next section, should be equally effective in ensuring peak engine performance and fuel economy.

12.14 Checking the timing on the road

The static or stroboscopic setting should be regarded only as the starting point for a series of road tests during which the timing can be precisely adjusted by rotating the distributor a fraction of a turn at a time to suit the condition of the engine and the fuel that will normally be used.

Tools: Spanner. Stop-watch.

1 Make a series of tests on a level road. Note carefully, by stop-watch readings, the time taken to accelerate from 30 mph to 50 mph in top gear, with the throttle fully open in each case and over the same stretch of road. The best ignition setting is that which results in the shortest time to accelerate over the speed range. This will also give the most economical fuel consumption.

2 When altering the timing by the roadside, move the distributor by only a fraction of a turn. Be particularly careful not to over-advance the ignition.

13 The transmission
Clutch, gearbox, propeller shaft, rear axle

All the Renault 12 models have front-wheel drive, the combined transmission and final-drive unit being mounted behind the engine. Synchromesh gearboxes are fitted as standard, with automatic transmission available as an option at extra cost.

When a synchromesh transmission is fitted the drive is taken from the engine through a cable-operated clutch to the synchromesh gears, and then back to the final-drive and differential pinions into which the front-wheel drive shafts are splined. Each shaft has a universal joint at its inner and outer end.

An automatic transmission is driven by a torque converter and gear changes are brought about by epicyclic gears and hydraulically-operated clutches and brakes, the timing of the changes being determined by an electronic computer which responds to engine speed and load.

The computer can be overriden by the gear selector, however, which provides a first gear 'hold' position and also allows changes to be made automatically between first and second gear – but not top gear – when set at 2. Fully automatic operation in all three gears is obtained only with the selector at A or D.

Transmission overhauls

For the benefit of the novice it should perhaps be explained that overhaul of the transmission components, or at least the major assemblies, calls for the use of special tools and gauges and it is for this reason that it is the practice, in many garages nowadays, to fit service-exchange assemblies, rather than to carry out major repairs to worn or defective units.

A complete overhaul of a synchromesh gearbox, for example, is beyond the scope of the average owner. Special service tools will be needed to do the job properly, and it will probably be necessary to renew the majority of the parts in a worn gearbox – which is something that you will only find out, of course, after you have stripped the box!

As we suggest in Chapter 8, there may be little difference between the total cost of the spares needed and the price of an exchange gearbox, with everything in favour of the professionally-rebuilt unit.

Work on an automatic gearbox and torque converter is also outside the province of the d.i.y. owner. Your local Renault dealer should have the large number of special tools and gauges which are required, and also – of even greater importance – the specialized knowledge which is needed to diagnose and correct the faults that may develop in these components.

The time factor

Where a routine maintenance job such as topping-up the oil in the transmission is concerned, the time factor must obviously depend on whether or not the work can be done quickly and conveniently with the car over a pit or raised on a garage lift or whether one has to wriggle under the side of the car and do the job the hard way!

As regards more ambitious work that is likely to be tackled at home, the following are some estimated times: clutch adjustment, 20 min; fitting a new clutch driven plate and/or clutch cover assembly (including removing and refitting the gearbox), 8 hr; removing and refitting gearbox or automatic transmission, 7 hr; removing and refitting one drive shaft, 2 hr.

The clutch

The clutch is a good example of the repair-by-replacement policy described earlier. Neither the clutch cover assembly nor the driven plate can be dismantled and both must be renewed as complete assemblies.

The clutch release mechanism is operated by a cable. Normally, the only maintenance needed is to check that there is a free movement of 10–20 mm (about ⅜–¾ in.) at the clutch pedal, before the weight of the clutch spring is felt. This will gradually decrease as the clutch friction-lining wears, and occasional adjustment to the length of the clutch-operating cable will therefore be needed, as described below.

13.1 Adjusting the clutch-operating cable

An adjusting nut is provided at the lower end of the cable where it is attached to the clutch operating lever.

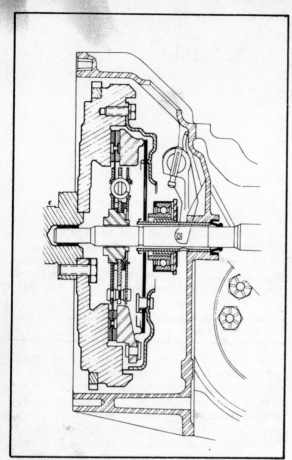

Fig. 13.1 A section through the clutch. Although an earlier pattern was superseded by a model which had different calibration tolerances, the general arrangement of both clutches is similar to that illustrated.

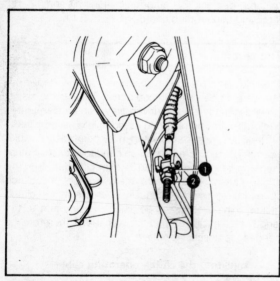

Fig. 13.2 Clutch adjustment is carried out at the lower end of the cable by turning the adjusting nut 1, after slackening the lock-nut 2.

To adjust the cable –

Tools: Spanners.

1 Loosen the lock-nut (the outer of the two nuts) and screw the adjusting nut along the threaded rod to give a free movement of 2–3 mm (just under ⅛ in.) at the lower end of the lever. This can be checked by pressing the lever back until the resistance of the main clutch spring is felt and then pulling it forward against the adjusting nut.

2 Tighten the lock-nut and check the free movement.

13.2 Clutch overhaul

Two different types of clutch have been fitted – the 170 DB 275 pattern and the 170 DB 310. The assemblies differ in their calibration tolerances and in some cases the later clutch must be fitted instead of the earlier pattern when replacing a worn unit. It is important, therefore, to consult your Renault dealer when buying a replacement clutch assembly.

Although it is sometimes sufficient to renew a worn driven plate alone (if this has failed after a fairly low mileage, for example), in practice it is a worthwhile insurance against future trouble to renew both the plate and the cover assembly at the same time. It is also advisable to renew the clutch release bearing.

To remove and refit the clutch assembly –

Materials: New parts as required. Paraffin. Rags. Marking paint or scriber. Loctite normal compound.
Tools: Spanners. Pliers. Screwdriver. Alignment tool (see item 6).

1 Remove the gearbox as described in Section 13.8.

2 If the clutch cover assembly is to be refitted, mark the flange of the cover and the flywheel to ensure reassembly in the same relative positions.

3 Unscrew the cover retaining screws progressively in a diagonal sequence to release the tension of the spring without distorting the cover flange. If you find balancing washers under some of the screws, make a note of their positions if the old parts are to be refitted. Otherwise discard them. Remove the cover and driven plate.

4 Clean the driven plate and the clutch assembly, brushing or blowing out any clutch dust from the latter (*don't inhale the dust*). Do not swill the cover in a paraffin bath, as this will remove the essential lubricant from the cover assembly.

5 Check the diaphragm spring in the cover assembly for any signs of wear or fractures and the driven plate for worn linings and loose or broken compression springs and worn hub splines. If oil has reached the driven plate, the rear main crankshaft bearing may be worn or the oil seal may be faulty. These items are normally dealt with during an engine overhaul. Oil can also leak past a worn gearbox first-motion shaft seal.

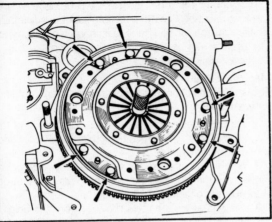

Fig. 13.3 When assembling the clutch to the flywheel, the bolts shown by the arrows must be tightened progressively. A centralizing mandrel for the driven plate is shown at the centre of the diaphragm spring.

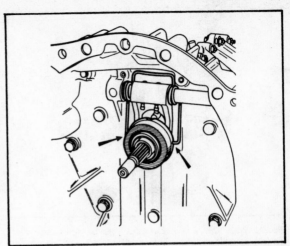

13.4 The clutch release bearing is retained by the hooked ends of the spring.

Fitting a new seal is described in Section 13.5. If the spigot bearing in the end of the crankshaft (into which the first-motion shaft of the gearbox fits) is worn, it should be renewed as described in Chapter 9, Section 9.20. If the flywheel is worn or scored, it can be removed by unscrewing the fixing bolts. *These are self-locking and must not be re-used.* New bolts must be fitted when reassembling. If the flywheel is not too deeply scored your Renault dealer will be able to reface it. Otherwise it will be necessary to fit a new flywheel.

6 When refitting the clutch, it is essential to centralize the hub of the driven plate. An improvised aligning tool can be made up from a length of wooden dowel, built up to the correct diameters to fit the spigot bearing in the flywheel and the bore of the clutch hub by wrapping it with insulating tape or masking tape.

7 With the aligning tool in place, and with the deeper side of the splined hub of the driven plate facing the gearbox, refit the clutch cover assembly. Before tightening the retaining screws progressively in a diagonal sequence, make sure that everything is properly lined-up, including the alignment marks and any balancing washers if the old cover is being refitted.

8 Refit the gearbox as described in Section 13.8.

13.3 Fitting a new clutch withdrawal bearing

Materials and tools: as for gearbox removal (Section 13.8).

1 Remove the gearbox as described in Section 13.8.

2 Unhook the springs from the withdrawal bearing and remove the bearing. Lubricate the bearing guide and the fingers of the fork with molybdenum disulphide grease and fit the new bearing, making sure that the ends of the springs are properly seated in the holes in the bearing carrier and in the fork. Also lightly grease the area on the diaphragm spring which contacts the withdrawal bearing.

13.4 Fitting a new clutch cable

To renew a broken or frayed cable –

Materials: New cable. Molybdenum disulphide grease.
Tools: Spanners. Pliers. Screwdriver. Jack. Axle stand.

1 Disconnect the cable from the clutch-operating lever and remove the bolts securing the mounting pad.

2 Remove the parcel tray, if necessary, and pull off the spring clip that retains the clutch pedal on the shaft. Push the shaft to the right to free the pedal.

3 Unhook the return spring and remove the pin which secures the fork end of the cable to the pedal. Detach the cable from the sleeve stop on the pedal bracket and remove it.

4 When fitting the new cable, lubricate the bore of the pedal and the fork-end retaining pin with molybdenum disulphide grease and adjust the free movement of the clutch operating lever as described in Section 13.1.

13.5 Renewing the gearbox first-motion shaft oil seal

We have treated this as a clutch job because the seal is fitted in a recess at the rear of the guide in the clutch housing through which the first motion shaft of the gearbox passes. The seal can be renewed during a clutch overhaul or when the gearbox has been separated from the engine.

Materials: New seal. Adhesive tape.
Tools: As for Section 13.2.

1 Separate the clutch housing from the gearbox.

2 Prise out the oil seal and fit the new seal, being careful not to damage it.

3 Cover the splines on the end of the first-motion shaft with adhesive tape before refitting the clutch housing, to avoid any risk of the splines cutting the lip of the seal.

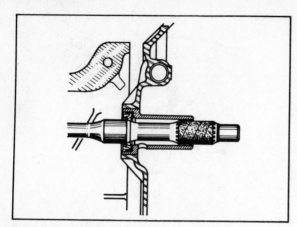

Fig 13.5 When fitting a new oil seal to the gearbox first-motion shaft the splines on the shaft must be wrapped with adhesive tape as shown, to prevent damage to the seal.

4 When refitting the clutch housing to the gearbox, use a new gasket and coat both sides with gasket cement.

The synchromesh gearbox

A synchromesh gearbox needs no attention, other than checking the oil-level during routine servicing, topping-up if necessary with EP80 gear oil and draining and refilling during the 6000–9000-mile service. Any oil leaks will be obvious while this is being done. If they are serious, ask your dealer for advice.

When trouble develops in the gearbox, considerable experience is needed to diagnose it with any degree of certainty. Excessive noise, or a tendency to jump out of gear, are usually caused by the cumulative effect of wear at a number of points, over a large mileage. Piecemeal replacements are seldom effective for very long; usually the most economical course is to fit a reconditioned gearbox.

13.6 Checking the oil level in a synchromesh gearbox

The level is checked by removing the combined filler and level plug from the left-hand side of the gearbox.
1 Clean the area around the plug and unscrew the plug.
2 If oil does not flow from the plug hole, inject a little EP80 gear oil from a squeeze-bottle with a flexible spout. Wait for the overflow to stop before replacing the plug.

13.7 Draining and refilling a synchromesh gearbox

The drain plug is in the underside of the transmission case. The combined filler and level plug is on the right-hand side. Both plugs have 10 mm square heads and the best tool to use is the Renault double-ended wrench B.Vi.380-1, which also fits the engine drain plug.

To inject oil into the filler hole it will be necessary to use a squeeze-bottle with a flexible spout or something similar. Change the oil after a reasonably long run, when the gearbox will be thoroughly warmed-up and the oil will flow freely.

Materials: EP80 gear oil.
Tools: 10 mm spanner or adjustable spanner. Container for waste oil.

1 With the car on a level surface, clean around the plugs and remove them, positioning a suitable container beneath the drain plug.
2 When oil ceases to drip from the drain plug opening, replace the plug and inject 3–3½ pints (1.7–2 litres) of EP80 gear oil into the level plug hole.
3 Check that oil is not overflowing from the hole. If the level is slightly too high, wait until the flow stops before replacing the plug.

13.8 Removing and refitting the gearbox

The gearbox can be removed without disturbing the engine, after the inner ends of the driving shafts have been disconnected from the sun wheels as described in Section 13.15.

Materials: Any new parts found to be necessary. Gearbox oil. Molybdenum disulphide grease.
Tools: Spanners. Pliers. Screwdriver. Jack. Axle stands. Special tool Sus.21 (not essential – see item 5).

1 Apart from disconnecting the drive shafts it will also be necessary to disconnect the battery, remove the starter motor, disconnect the clutch cable and remove its bracket. The speedometer cable must be disconnected from the gearbox and also the bolt on the gearshift control rod and the nut which secures the exhaust pipe to the gearbox-transmission rear cross-member.

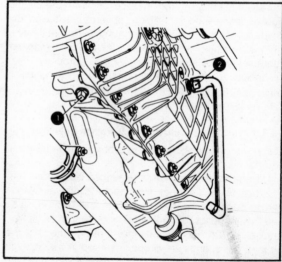

Fig. 13.6 The underside of a synchromesh transmission, showing the oil drain plug 1 and the filler and level plug 2. The useful Renault tool illustrated also fits the engine sump drain plug.

2 At this stage unscrew the three top bolts which secure the gearbox to the engine.

3 Place a jack under the rear end of the gearbox and take the weight of the assembly before unscrewing the three bolts which secure the cross-member to the gearbox and the two nuts which attach the ends of the cross-member to the side-members. Remove the cross-member.

4 Unscrew the five bolts which attach the side reinforcements and the clutch shield and the two bottom nuts which attach the gearbox to the engine.

5 It is now necessary to tilt the gearbox and the engine over to the left as viewed from the rear, until the side reinforcement touches the tubular cross-member. Renault dealers generally use the special spring compressor Sus.21 to pull the side of the engine down, hooking the top jaw of the tool on the lower edge of the cylinder block and lodging the lower end beneath the tubular cross-member and the anti-roll bar, but when a spring compressor is not available the same effect can be obtained by jacking up under the right-hand side of the engine, being careful, of course, to locate the jack so there is no possibility of causing any damage.

6 When the side reinforcement is in contact with the cross-member, ease the gearbox backwards, being careful not to allow any weight to be carried by the first-motion shaft of the gearshaft, as this will damage the clutch and may bend the shaft.

7 When refitting the gearbox, lubricate the first-motion shaft splines, and the splines in the sun wheels into which the drive shafts fit, with molybdenum disulphide grease. Don't use too much grease on the first-motion shaft splines. Make sure that the clutch driven plate is properly centralized as described in Section 13.2 and refer to Section 13.15 when reconnecting the drive-shaft joints.

8 The remainder of the reassembly is a reversal of the dismantling sequence. When reconnecting the gearshift control rod, select fourth gear and without holding the gear lever, tighten the control rod bolt. Don't forget to adjust the free movement of the clutch-operating lever and to refill the gearbox with oil.

The automatic transmission

As we emphasized at the beginning of this chapter, automatic transmission overhauls are jobs for specialists and this also applies to most checks and adjustments. A Renault dealer, for example, will have specialized test equipment, including an oil-pressure gauge to check the hydraulic circuit, an electrical temperature probe which can be inserted in the dipstick hole, and a sophisticated electrical control box which enables the governor, computer, solenoid ball valves and electrical wiring to be checked systematically.

Remember, however, that there is a 5-amp fuse in the fuse box which protects the transmission electrical circuits and if this should blow, the transmission will remain in third (top) gear. Always check for a blown fuse before assuming that repair or adjustment is required.

There are, however, one or two checks and adjustments which the average owner may have to carry out, such as the governor setting, which will be needed whenever the control wire has been disconnected during removing and refitting the carburettor, valve cover or cylinder head. This adjustment must be made in conjunction with adjustments to the accelerator cable and the kick-down switch, as all three are interdependent.

It may also be necessary to check the starter inhibitor switch.

Routine maintenance of the transmission is normally confined to checking the fluid level during the 3000-mile service and draining and refilling with fresh transmission fluid at 18 000-mile intervals.

The transmission must not be overfilled, as this causes abnormal overheating, but if the car is to be towed with the front wheels on the road, an extra 3½ pints (2 litres) should be added to provide adequate lubrication, since the oil pump in the transmission functions only when the engine is running. The distance of the tow must not exceed 30 miles and the road speed must be kept to less than 20 mph. Otherwise an automatic model must be towed with the front wheels off the ground.

13.9 Checking the fluid level in an automatic transmission.

The oil level should be checked at 3000-mile intervals with the car standing on a level surface. The engine must be running and the selector should be at P. The dipstick is beside the gearbox and the oil must be poured in through the dipstick tube, using a funnel.

If the level is checked with the transmission cold, it should be between notches 1 and 2 in Fig. 13.7. If the transmission is hot (after a run of several miles) the level should be between notches 2 and 3. Never overfill the transmission or allow the level to drop below the notch 1 or 2 as the case may be.

13.10 Draining and refilling an automatic transmission

The transmission must be drained and refilled at

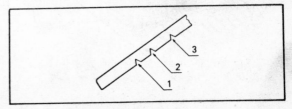

Fig. 13.7 The automatic transmission dipstick
With gearbox cold: 1, minimum mark; 2, maximum mark.
With gearbox hot: 2, minimum mark; 3, maximum mark.

18 000-mile intervals, when the oil is hot and immediately after stopping the engine, to ensure that any impurities are held in suspension in the oil

The transmission, including the torque converter, contains about 9 pints (5 litres) of oil but only about 5½–6½ pints (3–4 litres) is needed to refill the transmission after draining it in service, since the remainder of the oil is trapped in the torque converter.

Materials: Elf Renaultmatic or Mobil ATF 200 automatic transmission fluid.

Tools: Spanners. Container for waste oil.

1 Remove the dipstick.

2 Remove the drain plug shown in Fig. 13.8. Some transmissions have only one plug.

3 Allow the oil to drain for about 5 minutes before replacing the drain plug.

4 Refill the transmission with about 5½–6½ pints (3–4 litres) of the correct oil, by pouring the oil into the dipstick tube.

5 Check the oil level with the dipstick as described for a 'cold' transmission in Section 13.9 and top-up the level if necessary.

13.11 Adjusting the governor setting

This adjustment must be carried out whenever the control cable has been disconnected, either at the carburettor end or at the transmission end.

Tools: Spanners. Pliers. Rule.

1 Screw the stop-nut on the sleeve at the governor end of the cable to the centre of the thread and attach the end of the cable to the control quadrant – see Fig. 13.9.

2 Connect the other end of the cable to the cam on the carburettor, if necessary (Fig. 13.9).

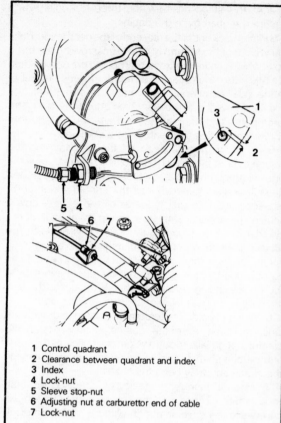

1 Control quadrant
2 Clearance between quadrant and index
3 Index
4 Lock-nut
5 Sleeve stop-nut
6 Adjusting nut at carburettor end of cable
7 Lock-nut

13.9 Adjusting the governor setting on an automatic transmission. Full details are given in Section 13.11.

3 Depress the accelerator fully and tension the inner cable by moving the sleeve at the carburettor end of the cable to take up the slack in the inner cable. Secure the sleeve in this position.

4 Release the accelerator pedal and tighten the sleeve stop-nut at the governor end of the cable about one turn.

5 Check the adjustment between the quadrant and the index shown in Fig. 13.9, with the accelerator again fully depressed. It should be 0.2–0.7 mm (0.008–0.028 in.). If necessary readjust the stop-nut and finally tighten the lock-nut.

13.12 Adjusting the accelerator cable and kick-down switch

The kick-down switch is integral with the accelerator cable and is operated when the accelerator is depressed beyond the normal full-throttle position. Correct adjustment is important to ensure correct operation of the automatic transmission.

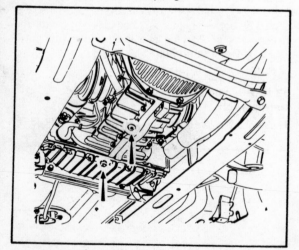

Fig. 13.8 The arrows show two drain plugs which may be fitted to the underside of an automatic transmission. When draining the transmission only the rear plug should be removed.

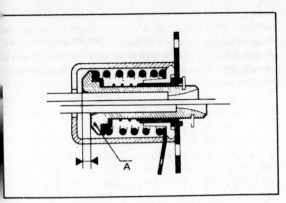

Fig. 13.10 Adjusting the accelerator cable and kick-down switch. Free movement of the stop sleeve A should be 3-4 mm (⅛-⁵/₃₂ in.).

Tools: Spanners. Pliers. Rule.

1 Make sure that the choke is fully open and depress the accelerator pedal through its maximum travel. Wedge it in this position if an assistant is not available.

2 Check that there is sufficient initial play in the cable to allow the stop sleeve shown in Fig. 13.10 to move 3–4 mm (⅛–⁵/₃₂ in.).

3 If it is necessary to adjust the accelerator cable, remember that the governor control cable must also be checked as described in Section 13.11.

4 If the switch does not operate when correctly adjusted, check it by disconnecting the wire from the terminal and connecting a test bulb between this terminal and the positive battery terminal. The lamp should light up whenever the accelerator pedal is fully depressed.

13.13 Checking the starter inhibitor switch

This switch prevents the engine from being started when the gear selector is placed in any position except N (Neutral) or P (Park). It is attached to the rear face of the selector quadrant (the end nearest the front seats) and is accessible when the cover over the selector mechanism has been lifted. The switch is not repairable or adjustable and if it is faulty a new one must be fitted.

13.14 Removing and refitting an automatic transmission

The automatic transmission can be removed from below without disturbing the engine.

It is a heavy unit and Renault dealers normally use a special jacking fixture but an ordinary jack can be used, with suitable padding to avoid any risk of damaging the underside of the transmission. It is also advisable to enlist the help of an assistant during the actual removal process.

To prevent the torque converter being disconnected from the transmission during removal and refitting, make up a clamp by drilling a hole in a short strip of steel to take one of the transmission retaining bolts.

Materials: Any spares found to be necessary. Automatic transmission fluid – 9 pints (5 litres) if torque converter has been drained, otherwise 4½ pints (2.5 litres).
Tools: Spanners. Sockets. Converter clamping strip. Two jacks. Axle stands.

Removing the transmission –

1 Drain the transmission. Remember that if the car has recently been run the oil may be hot enough to burn the fingers.

2 Disconnect the battery and the transmission wiring harness. Take off the starter motor.

3 Free the inner ends of the drive shafts from the sun wheels as described in Section 13.15.

4 Remove the anti-roll bar and the tubular cross-member and disconnect the exhaust downpipe from the manifold and at its mounting under the transmission support, so that it will not obstruct the removal of the transmission.

5 Unscrew the top bolts which attach the transmission to the engine and remove the two fixing studs by screwing two nuts on to the end of a stud and locking one against the other.

6 Remove the converter shield and place a jack beneath the transmission, with suitable padding to protect the underside.

7 Take off the rear transmission cross-member and lower the transmission with the jack. Disconnect the governor cable, the vacuum capsule pipe and the selector control. Before doing this move the selector lever in the driving compartment to the first-gear hold position and disconnect the rod at the computer and at the selector lever end by unscrewing the clamping bolt.

8 Carefully ease the transmission away and as soon as it has been disconnected, clamp a retaining plate against the converter by using one of the transmission retaining bolts.

Refitting the transmission. This is a reversal of dismantling but the following points must be borne in mind –

1 The converter plate fixing holes in the crankshaft are not drilled symmetrically and the converter can therefore be fitted only in one position. Lubricate the white-metal bush and the face of the seal at the transmission end of the converter with automatic transmission fluid and the bush in the crankshaft with molybdenum disulphide grease.

2 Make sure that the locating dowels for the transmission are in place.

3 *Align the driving plate so that the three fixing holes are in line with the three bosses on the converter.* It is essential to check this before the transmission retaining bolts are tightened, otherwise the converter plate may be distorted.

4 The three converter fixing bolts must be inserted but not fully tightened until the converter has been turned so that the spot of blue paint near the centre is at

the bottom. Tighten the fixing bolts which are accessible in this position to 25 lb ft (35 Nm) and then turn the assembly to tighten the last bolt to the same torque.

5 The nuts on the anti-roll bar bearings and links should not be fully tightened until the wheels are carrying the weight of the front of the car, either by lowering them to the ground or on to suitable blocks.

6 Check the adjustments described in Section 13.11 and 13.12.

The drive shafts

Several different types of drive shaft have been fitted to the various models and these can be identified from Fig. 13.11. The protected TE type of shaft can be fitted only to cars which have modified lower front suspension arms but the Spider GE 86 coupling can be fitted to all models, whether the earlier or the later types of suspension arms are used – but in any event it is advisable to obtain the advice of your Renault dealer when replacements are necessary.

The drive shaft joints on Renault 12 models do not seem to give much trouble – especially when the later assemblies are fitted – but when they do eventually wear, as will be revealed by clicking or knocking when the car is driven slowly around the corner on full lock, replacement of the complete drive shaft and coupling assembly will be needed.

The life of the joints largely depends on how the car is driven. Fierce acceleration and a lot of use in traffic and on winding roads will tend to shorten their lives.

13.15 Removing and refitting a drive shaft

This is a straightforward job, but the method used will

depend on whether or not a special tool T.Av.509 is available. This is a strut which is placed between the shock-absorber lower mounting in the upper arm and the hinge pin for the lower suspension arm as shown in Fig. 13.12 to prevent the spring forcing the upper suspension arm downwards. A similar strut could be made from angle-iron or I-section iron bar, with a Vee cut at each end. The length should just fit between the lower shock-absorber mounting and the lower suspension arm pivot when the front wheels are carrying the weight of the car and the driving shafts are horizontal.

If these struts are not available, however, all is not lost since an alternative method can be used to free the upper suspension arm from the stub-axle carrier. In this case you will need a strong lever, such as a crowbar or a short section of scaffold pole, and a wooden block to prevent the lever damaging the upper suspension arm.

Materials: Any new parts required. Molybdenum disulphide grease. Special Renault sealer for roll pins.

Tools: Spanners or sockets. Pin punch to fit the roll pins at the inner end of the drive shaft (preferably B.Vi.31-01). Ball-pin separator. Length of bar to prevent wheel hub rotating, or special tool Rou.436-01. Also, if drive shaft is to be detached from hub, special tool T.Av.235 or soft metal drift and hammer, and T.Av. 236 (essential). Jack. Axle stands.

First we will describe the method used if the special spacer strut T.Av.509 is available –

1 Jack-up under the lower suspension arm sufficiently to allow the strut to be put in between the lower shock-absorber mounting – between the upper arm and the anti-roll bar link – and the pivot for the lower suspension arm.

Coupling at wheel end	Coupling at gearbox end	Vehicle type
Cast "BED"  then Cast protected "T.E." 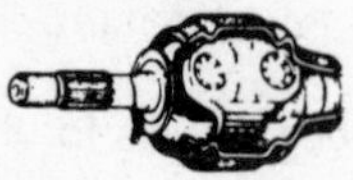	GI 62 	R.1170 R.1171 R.1177 R.1330
"Spider GE 86" 	 GI 69	R.1337

Fig. 13.11 The different types of drive shaft which may be fitted can be identified from these drawings.

2 Jack-up under the side-member and support the car really securely by an axle stand. Apply the handbrake firmly. Remove the wheel.

3 Slacken the axle nut. This is very tight. If an assistant is available, get him to apply the brakes as firmly as possible while you slacken the nut, using a well-fitting socket and a strong handle. If you are working alone, lodge a length of strong steel bar or angle iron between two of the wheel nuts, with the end resting on the ground or a suitable support. Do not lodge it between the unprotected wheel studs, as this will damage the threads. Renault dealers use a special tool, Rou.436-01 and if you can hire this, so much the better.

4 Slacken, but do not remove, the nuts on the steering arm ball joint and the upper suspension arm ball joint and use the ball-pin separator to unlock the joints.

5 Punch out the roll pins from the coupling at the inner end of the shaft.

6 Remove the brake caliper (see Chapter 15), without disconnecting the brake hose and support it so that the hose will not be strained.

7 Unscrew the nuts and disconnect the upper suspension arm and steering arm joints.

8 Lower the hub on the lower suspension arm so that the drive shaft slides out of the gearbox and then temporarily reconnect the steering arm ball joint.

9 If necessary, disconnect the outer joint from the hub. This may not always be needed — for example when removing the gearbox or automatic transmission.

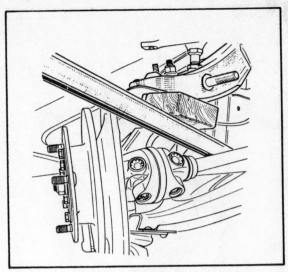

Fig. 13.13 Using a lever and a wooden block to raise the upper suspension arm in order to free the ball joint from the stub axle carrier when a spacer strut (Fig. 13.12) is not available.

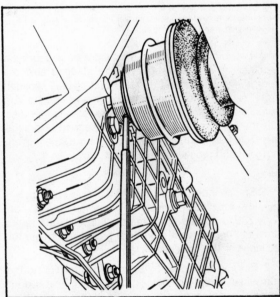

Fig. 13.14 Punching out the roll pin which secures the inner coupling.

Preferably use the special tool T.Av.235 to push the drive shaft out of the hub. If you tap it out, use a soft metal drift and be careful not to damage the threads on the shaft.

10 Finally, remove the steering arm ball joint nut and withdraw the shaft.

To remove the drive shaft when the special spacer strut is not available —

The general dismantling is as just described but in order to free the upper suspension arm from the stub-axle carrier, remove the nut from the upper suspension

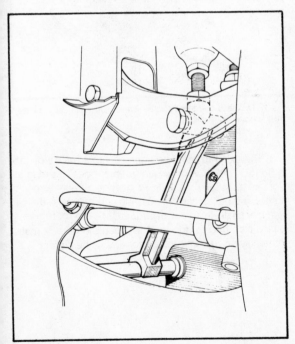

Fig. 13.12 A strut fitted between the lower shock absorber mounting and the lower suspension arm pivot to support the upper arm. The example shown is the Renault special tool T.Av.509 but a substitute could be made from angle-iron.

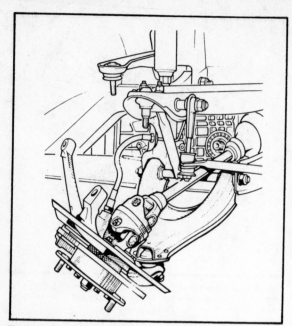

Fig. 13.15 The stub axle carrier can be tilted downwards when the upper ball joints have been released, allowing the drive shaft to be disconnected from the transmission.

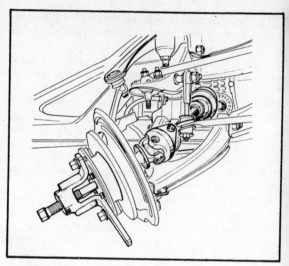

Fig. 13.16 Using the special puller T.Av.235 to push the drive shaft out of the hub.

arm ball joint after freeing the taper with a ball-pin extractor, and also disconnect the steering arm ball joint, without removing its nut. Then place a wooden block beneath the upper suspension arm and insert a lever between the block and the lower side-member. Lift the lever to raise the upper suspension arm sufficiently to free the ball joint. Disconnect the steering arm ball joint and proceed as described above.

To refit the drive shaft –

1 Smear the splines of the stub axle with molybdenum disulphide grease and use the special tool T.Av.236 to pull the shaft into the hub. Any attempt to drive the hub on with a drift will probably damage the bearings or the universal joint.

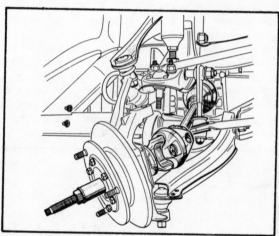

Fig. 13.17 The special tool T.Av.236 should be used to pull the drive shaft into position in the hub.

2 Position the drive shaft correctly in relation to the sun wheel in the gearbox or transmission and slide it home. After reconnecting the suspension and steering arm ball joints (using a lever to lift the upper arm if the spacer strut has not been fitted) fit two new roll pins, preferably using the special drift B.Vi.31-01, and seal the ends of the pins with the special Renault sealer.

3 The axle nut must be tightened to a torque of 115 lb ft (156 Nm). If your torque wrench does not read as high as this (or if you don't have a torque wrench) tighten the nut as hard as possible and then take the car to a Renault dealer to have it torqued to the correct figure.

Don't forget to top-up the gearbox or automatic transmission to compensate for any oil being lost.

14 The suspension and steering

Satisfactory steering and good tyre life depend on the condition of the suspension and steering gear, and also on the maintenance of the correct steering 'geometry', which can be upset by quite a minor kerb collision.

Steering geometry checks must be left to a Renault dealer, and should preferably be carried out at 6000–9000-mile intervals (especially if the rate of wear on the front tyres seems suspiciously high).

The alignment of the front wheels can be altered by adjusting the steering rack end fittings – but here again it is best to have the checks made by a dealer.

Wheel-wobble and quite severe vibration at about 40–50 mph and 60–80 mph – sometimes at lower speeds – can be caused by unbalanced wheels and tyres.

It is advisable to have the wheel balance checked by a properly equipped garage every 6000 miles, preferably with the aid of a dynamic balancer which allows the degree of unbalance to be checked electronically when the wheel is spun.

The rear wheels should be balanced at the same time. They can not only cause vibration, but may cause a rear-end steering effect if they are badly out of balance.

The suspension

The front suspension takes the form of upper and lower suspension arms, between which the stub-axle carrier swivels on ball joints. The lower arm has widely-spaced pivots at its inner end while the upper arm is located in a fore-and-aft direction by a tie-rod.

The load is taken by a coil spring which surrounds a telescopic hydraulic damper, the upper end of the spring being located in a housing on the underside of the wheel arch and the lower end resting in a cup which is welded to the damper. The lower end of the damper is connected to the upper suspension arm by a rubber-bushed pin.

An anti-roll bar is coupled by rubber-bushed links to the upper suspension arms.

The stub-axle carrier ball joints and the ball joint which connects the steering arm to the carrier are lubricated on assembly and normally need no further attention, apart from regular checks to make sure that the grease-retaining gaiters have not been dislodged or damaged.

A 'dead' rear axle is used. The axle beam that carries the rear-wheel hubs and brake assemblies is fabricated from steel pressings and is located by a trailing side arm at each end and by a central upper arm in the form of a pivoted A-bracket.

The load is carried by coil springs, with telescopic dampers fitted inside them.

The time factor

Suggested times for the more important suspension jobs are: Renewing an upper suspension ball joint, 1 hr; renewing a lower ball joint, 2 hr; removing and refitting the stub-axle carrier assembly, 2 hr; checking and adjusting the rear-wheel bearings (one side), 45 min; removing and refitting the dampers (rear pair), 1½ hr.

14.1 Renewing an upper ball joint or rubber boot

Before an upper ball joint can be renewed, the pin of the joint must be freed from the upper suspension arm. To do this either the special spacer strut T.Av.509, or a home-made substitute, is required. Alternatively, a strong lever and a block of wood can be used. The method of freeing the joint is fully described in Chapter 13, Section 13.15 and need not be repeated here.

Materials: New joint or boot. Special grease, obtainable from a Renault dealer.

Tools: Jack. Axle stands. Spanners. Ball-pin extractor. Spacer strut or lever. Electric drill. Torque wrench.

1 Jack-up the front of the side of the car and support it on an axle stand. Remove the wheel.

2 Free the upper ball joint from the suspension arm as described in Chapter 13, Section 13.15.

3 If the joint is serviceable and only the rubber boot is to be renewed, remove the old boot, wipe the joint

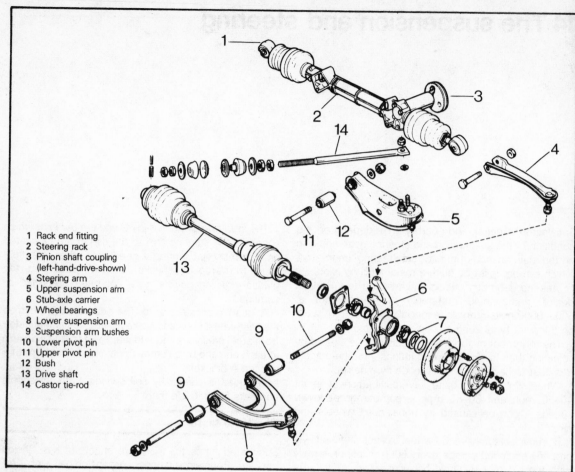

1 Rack end fitting
2 Steering rack
3 Pinion shaft coupling
  (left-hand-drive-shown)
4 Steering arm
5 Upper suspension arm
6 Stub-axle carrier
7 Wheel bearings
8 Lower suspension arm
9 Suspension arm bushes
10 Lower pivot pin
11 Upper pivot pin
12 Bush
13 Drive shaft
14 Castor tie-rod

Fig. 14.1 The componets of the front suspension and steering gear.

clean and half-fill the new boot with grease. Fit the plastic sleeve to the boot, slide the assembly into position and install the retaining ring, using a loop of string to pull the end into position.

4 If the joint is to be renewed, drill the heads of the two rivets and punch them out before removing the retaining bolt.

5 Fit the new joint, using the bolts supplied. If a support plate is supplied in the kit, fit this inside the suspension arm on the opposite side to the joint. Fit the new bolts, with their heads downwards, and tighten their nuts to 26 lb ft (35 Nm).

14.2 Changing a lower ball joint or boot

The lower suspension arm must be removed as described in Section 14.5 before the lower ball joint can be changed.
Materials and tools: as for Sections 14.1 and 14.5.

1 Remove the lower suspension arm as described in Section 14.5.

2 Change the boot or the joint as described in Section 14.1. The heads of the bolts must be towards the boot side of the joint.

14.3 Removing the stub-axle carrier and servicing the wheel bearings

The stub-axle carrier and the front hub and brake disc can be removed as an assembly by disconnecting the upper and lower ball joints and the drive shaft as described in Chapter 13, Section 13.15.

We suggest that this course be adopted when it is necessary to renew the bearings, and that the complete assembly should then be taken to a Renault dealer, since a proper bearing extractor and a press, with suitable distance pieces, should be used to remove and refit the bearings to avoid any risk of damaging the parts.

Refitting the assembly to the car is also described in Section 13.15 and as recommended in that section the special tool T.Av.236 should be used to draw the end of the drive shaft into the hub.

14.4 Removing and refitting an upper suspension arm

It is not necessary to disconnect the drive shaft before removing an upper arm and the only special tool required will be a ball-pin extractor.

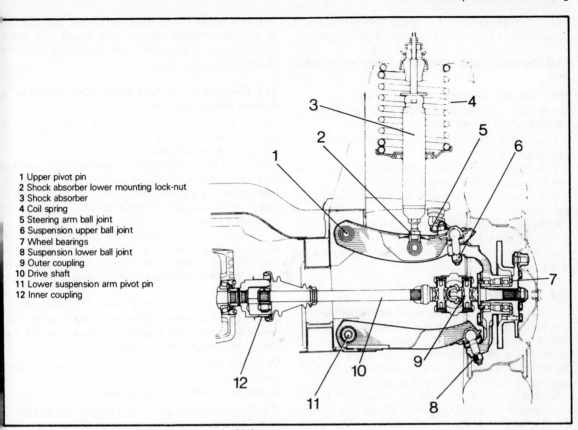

1 Upper pivot pin
2 Shock absorber lower mounting lock-nut
3 Shock absorber
4 Coil spring
5 Steering arm ball joint
6 Suspension upper ball joint
7 Wheel bearings
8 Suspension lower ball joint
9 Outer coupling
10 Drive shaft
11 Lower suspension arm pivot pin
12 Inner coupling

Fig. 14.2 A section through the front suspension and wheel hub.

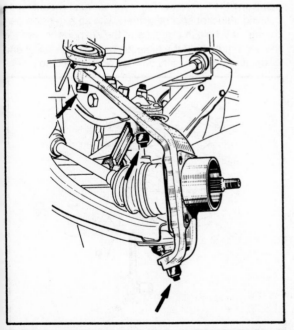

Fig. 14.3 The stub-axle carrier can be removed when a strut has been placed between the lower shock absorber mounting and the lower suspension arm pivot pin and the nuts shown by the arrows have been unscrewed.

Materials: Any new parts required to recondition the arm – ball joint, boot, rubber bushes.
Tools: Jack. Axle stand. Spanners. Ball-pin extractor. Hammer. Drift. Torque wrench.

1 Jack-up both front wheels and take off the wheel on the side on which the arm is to be removed.

2 Unlock the lock-nut on the bottom mounting of the shock absorber.

3 Disconnect the castor tie-rod from the suspension arm.

4 Remove the bottom mounting pin of the shock absorber.

5 Disconnect the upper ball joint from the swivel hub, using a ball-pin extractor. Remove the nut from the upper arm hinge pin and tap out the pin.

6 Lift the arm and unscrew the bottom mounting of the shock absorber by rotating the shock absorber.

7 When refitting the arm, smear the upper arm hinge pin and the shock absorber bottom mounting pin with grease. First screw on the shock absorber bottom mounting, then insert the upper ball joint pin and screw on the nut by several turns. Complete the reassembly without fully tightening the nut on the hinge pin, the shock absorber bottom mounting and the tie-rod. These nuts should be tightened to the correct torque only when the front wheels are carrying the weight of the

car. It may be convenient to lower the wheels on to suitable blocks to maintain a reasonable working height.

14.5 Removing and refitting a lower suspension arm

Materials: Any new parts required. Grease.
Tools: Jack. Axle stands. Spanners. Ball-pin extractor. Hammer. Drift. Torque wrench.

1 Break the taper on the lower ball-joint pin, using a ball-pin extractor.

2 Remove the hinge pin from the inner end of the arm by withdrawing it towards the front of the car.

3 Disconnect the lower ball joint from the hub carrier and remove the arm.

4 When reassembling, smear the hinge pin with grease. Do not tighten the nut on the ball joint and the hinge pin until the front wheels are carrying the weight of the car.

14.6 The castor tie-rods

The castor tie-rod fitted between the upper suspension arm and a bracket on the side-member on each side of the car determines the castor angle of the front wheel. The angle is adjusted by altering the length of the tie-rod at the bracket end, by slackening the lock-nuts and screwing the adjusting nuts along the rod.

Since this adjustment calls for the use of special wheel-alignment equipment, never disturb the nuts on the forward ends of the tie-rods unnecessarily. Adjustment must be carried out by a Renault dealer.

14.7 Renewing the rubber bushes in the suspension components

This job is quite straightforward when the suspension arms have been removed. A press or a vice can be used to force out the old bearings and install the new ones, using suitable distance pieces.

Where the vice jaws cannot be brought to bear effectively, a bolt or length of threaded rod, fitted with washers and lengths of tube, can be used with a nut to extract or fit a bush.

Before removing the bushes measure carefully the distance between the ends of the bushes in the lower suspension arms and the amount by which each bush protudes in the upper arms. This is important, to maintain the correct steering geometry when the parts are reassembled.

14.8 Removing and refitting a front spring and damper

The damper may be removed alone, or complete with the spring, but in either case special Renault tools should be used to avoid any risk of damage or injury during removal and dismantling. Another special tool will be needed to compress the spring before the assembly is refitted to the car.

In view of this, we suggest that the job should be left to a Renault dealer or that his advice should be obtained, and the correct tools borrowed or hired before tackling the work.

14.9 Removing and refitting a rear spring or a damper (shock absorber)

This job is quite straightforward. If only the spring is to be removed there is no need to disturb the upper mounting of the damper.

Since dampers are stored lying on their sides, air may enter their working chambers and upset their operation. Before fitting a damper, therefore, hold it upright and pump it until an even resistance to extending and compressing it builds up.

Unfortunately there is no way of checking a worn shock absorber without using specialized equipment but if the damper does not show an even, progressive resistance when extended and compressed, it should be renewed.

As will be seen from Figs. 14.6 and 14.7 there are two different arrangements for the upper and lower damper mounting bushes and washers, so make sure that you obtain the correct parts for your car.

Materials: New spring or damper, if required. New mounting rubbers.
Tools: Jack. Axle stand. Spanners.

1 Disconnect the upper mounting of the damper — this is not necessary if only the spring is to be removed.

2 Jack-up the side of the car and support it on an axle stand and then unscrew the lower damper mounting by passing a socket spanner, fitted with an extension bar, through the hole in the base of the suspension arm. At the same time hold the hexagon beneath the lower end of the damper stationary with an open-ended spanner.

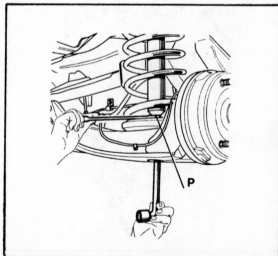

Fig. 14.4 Removing a rear spring or shock absorber. With the car supported the lower shock-absorber mounting nut can be unscrewed while the hexagon on the shaft P is held by an open-ended spanner.

3 Push the damper up as far as it will go and place a jack between the rear axle beam and the underside of the floor. Extend the jack to tilt the axle downwards sufficiently to allow the spring and shock absorber to be withdrawn.

4 When reassembling, first fit the shock absorber to its upper mounting, if this has been disconnected. Locate the bottom end of the spring – this has a *spiral* seating area as opposed to the flat area at the top – so that the end of the coil is located at the point in the lower cup shown in Fig. 14.8. Then fit the lower shock-absorber mounting, making sure that the cups are the right way round – see Fig. 14.6 or 14.7.

14.10 Removing and refitting the rear suspension side arms and upper arm

These jobs are quite straightforward, entailing only simple dismantling but when removing the side arms it will be necessary to remove the rear brake drums and disconnect the handbrake cable from the lever inside the brake and to free it from the backplate and from the side arm.

The rubber bushes can be changed as described in Section 14.7. When reassembling do not tighten the nuts on the hinge pins until the rear wheels are carrying the weight of the car. To maintain a reasonable working height, refit the wheels and lower them on to suitable blocks.

14.11 Removing, refitting and adjusting the rear-wheel bearings

The rear-wheel bearings are of the taper-roller type and when correctly adjusted should have an end-float of 0.01–0.05 mm (0.001–0.002 in.). This represents a just-perceptible movement when the wheel is pulled and pushed – not rocked – on its hub.

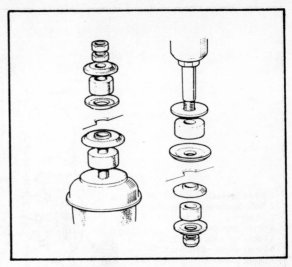

Fig. 14.6 The upper and lower rear shock-absorber mountings used when removable cups are fitted.

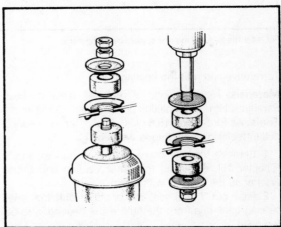

Fig. 14.7 The arrangement of the rear shock absorber mountings used with welded cups.

Fig. 14.5 With the shock-absorber lower mounting uncoupled the axle beam can be forced downwards with a jack and the spring and shock absorber removed.

Fig. 14.8 The rear spring lower mounting, showing the recess in the cup at A which locates the end of the bottom coil of the spring.

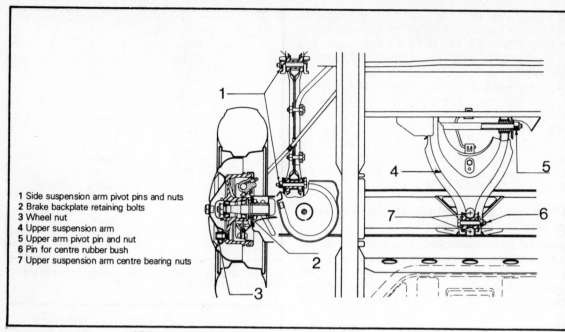

1 Side suspension arm pivot pins and nuts
2 Brake backplate retaining bolts
3 Wheel nut
4 Upper suspension arm
5 Upper arm pivot pin and nut
6 Pin for centre rubber bush
7 Upper suspension arm centre bearing nuts

Fig. 14.9 The layout of the rear suspension components.

To remove and refit the bearings —

Materials: New bearings, if required. New oil seal. Paraffin. Cloth. High-melting-point grease. Split-pin.
Tools: As for Section 15.6 plus special Renault bearing puller, feeler gauges, torque wrench.

1 Remove the rear brake drum and hub assembly (Chapter 15), extracting the outer bearing and thrust washer as the drum is withdrawn.

2 Prise out the oil seal and press or drift the inner bearing track ring from the hub, if the bearing is to be removed.

3 A suitable bearing puller will be needed to remove the taper-roller bearing from the stub axle, but this can be left in place if the assemblies are serviceable. Renault dealers use a special tool for the job (which depends on the diameter of the stub axle) and if you are doubtful about the condition of the bearings it will be better to allow your dealer to renew them.

4 Otherwise, clean the bearings carefully, pack them with grease, smear grease around the inside of the hub (but do not fill the recess) and fit a new oil seal.

5 Reassemble the hub and adjust the bearing end-float by tightening the axle nut to 22 lb ft (30 Nm), while rotating the drum. Unscrew the nut a quarter of a turn and check the end-float by inserting a feeler gauge between the rear face of the nut and the thrust washer.

6 When the clearance is correct, fit the nut-retaining sleeve so that one of its slots is aligned with the split-pin hole and fit a new split-pin.

7 Put about ¼ oz (10 g) of high-melting-point grease into the grease cap before refitting it.

The steering gear

The rack-and-pinion steering gear is bolted to a cross-member in the engine compartment. When the steering wheel is turned the movement is transmitted by the steering column to the pinion of the steering unit, which moves the rack from side to side. The ends of the rack are coupled to the steering arms, which in turn are connected to the stub-axle carriers by ball joints.

The rack and the rubber boots on the ball joints should be inspected during the 6000–9000-mile service to make sure that they have not been damaged. Pull the corrugations apart and look for cracks and splits. Apart from allowing lubricant to escape, a damaged boot or

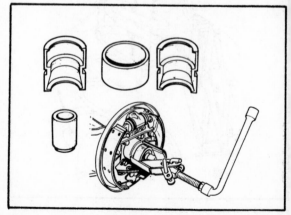

Fig. 14.10 Removing a rear hub inner bearing, using a special Renault extractor.

ellows will also allow water and grit to enter the joint or e rack, quickly rendering it unserviceable.

teering gear repairs

efore discussing steering gear repairs, one or two eneral points must be mentioned. The most important that many steering troubles can be attributed quite mply to incorrect wheel alignment, the wrong tyre ressures, unbalanced front wheels and tyres or weak ampers. As indicated at the beginning of this chapter, teering alignment checks and wheel balancing must be ft to a Renault dealer. It is useless to attempt to do nese jobs without the aid of specialized equipment.

Removing and refitting the rack-and-pinion assembly nust also be left to a Renault dealer, because it is ssential to adjust the steering box to the correct height nd parallelism when refitting it. This calls for the use of ery specialized equipment, including alignment auges.

Never be tempted, therefore, to slacken the four olts which retain the steering unit to the cross-member.

4.12 Servicing the steering arms and ball joints

he ball joints at the outer ends of the steering arms are ot repairable. If the joints are worn new arms must be tted.

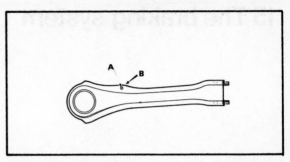

Fig. 14.11 The steering arms have a boss B which must face the front of the vehicle. In addition the left-hand arm may have an identifying hole A drilled in it.

A grease-retaining boot can be changed by easing out the old boot with a screwdriver, packing the new boot with grease and using a length of tube which has a 37 mm ($1^{15}/_{32}$ in.) bore to fit the new boot.

There is a boss on each steering arm (see Fig. 14.11) which must face forward and a hole may be drilled in the flange of the left-hand arm to identify it.

The hinge pins for the steering arms on later models, together with their nuts, have a 10 mm × 125 pitch thread instead of the 10 mm × 150 pitch thread used on early assemblies. Be careful not to mix the pins and nuts. The pins should be horizontal. If necessary slacken the lock-nut on the rack end fitting and align the pin correctly.

15 The braking system

Hydraulic four-wheel braking systems, in which fluid pressure is generated in a master cylinder when the brake pedal is depressed, are used on all models. The fluid pressure is transmitted through pipelines to pistons in 'slave' cylinders which operate the front and rear brakes.

The front wheels are fitted with disc brakes, in which the pistons force steel pads, faced with friction material, against the sides of a steel disc which is attached to the wheel hub. The rear-brake cylinders are mounted on the stationary backplate of each brake and the pistons force brake shoes into contact with the rotating drums.

A vacuum-servo, which reduces the effort required on the brake pedal, is provided as standard on the Renault 12 Estate, TS and later TL models.

The fluid pressure in the pipelines which serve the rear brakes is regulated by a load-sensitive valve, linked to the central pivoted bracket which locates the rear axle. Pressure in the rear brake cylinders is reduced when the car is lightly loaded, preventing premature locking of the rear wheels under heavy braking conditions, but increased pressure is applied when the rear wheels are carrying more weight.

Self-adjusting rear brakes are fitted to some models – see Section 15.7. Other refinements that may be incorporated are a tandem master cylinder supplying separate front and rear brake circuits, a pressure-drop indicator and a pressure-drop bypass unit.

Practical pointers

As with other components of the car, 'repair by replacement' is assuming increasing importance where braking systems are concerned. Service-exchange sets or relined brake shoes from a reputable supplier are a better proposition than attempting to reline existing shoes. Similarly, it is preferable to fit new master and slave cylinders instead of installing new rubber seals in the old components, in which the bores are likely to be worn, scored or corroded. Brake manufacturers, in fact, tend increasingly to supply only new or reconditioned assemblies, instead of repair kits.

This will explain why we have not included in th chapter detailed instructions for stripping or repairin any of the hydraulic components.

Now for one or two useful tips that apply to many the jobs described in this chapter –

Before disconnecting a brake pipe union, remove th filler cap from the fluid reservoir, place a sheet of thi plastic (which can be cut out from a plastic bag) over th opening and screw the cap firmly on to it. By preventin entry of air into the reservoir in this way the minimur amount of fluid will be lost when a union is discon nected. *Don't forget to remove the plastic when th work has been completed* – otherwise the brakes wi bind.

Better still, use a special brake-pipe clamp. Mos accessory shops sell these clamps, which enable a flex ible hose to be clamped-off without risk of damagin the walls of the tube, before a union is disconnected The use of a clamp will often avoid – or reduce – th need for bleeding the system after reassembly.

A Mole or similar self-locking wrench can be safel used as a clamp, provided that two curved pads ar fitted to the jaws. These can be made by cutting a shor length of 1½ in. diameter tube longitudinally and tapin the half-sections to the jaws so that the pipe will b pinched between the rounded, outer faces of the tube without the risk of cutting or crushing it.

The second point is that brake fluid acts as a ver efficient paint stripper – so be sure to keep it away fron the bodywork. Any drips or splashes should be wipe off immediately and the area washed with water and detergent.

The time factor

A complete check on the braking system can be carrie out comfortably in a morning. Typical times for othe individual jobs are: fitting new brake shoes to two drun brakes, 1½ hr; fitting a set of disc brake pads, 1 hr bleeding the brakes, 45 min; adjusting the rear brakes 20 min per brake.

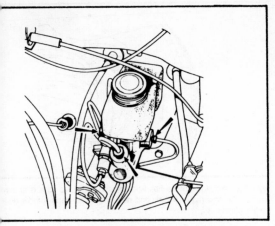

Fig. 15.1 A brake fluid reservoir which is divided into two sections. When topping-up, check the unions indicated for fluid leaks.

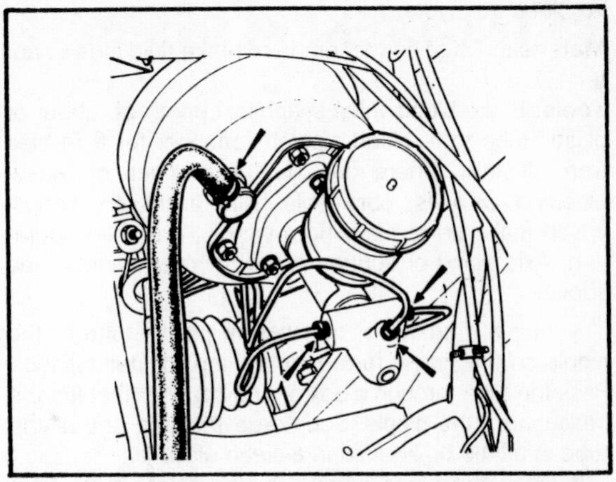

Fig. 15.2 A brake fluid reservoir mounted on the brake servo. Check the unions indicated by arrows for leaks and the tightness of the clip on the vacuum pipe.

Routine servicing

15.1 Topping-up the brake fluid reservoir

This is largely a precautionary check. If frequent topping-up is needed, look for fluid leakage from the pipelines, unions or hydraulic cylinders. Since brake fluid specifications change from time to time (to take advantage of improved technology) ask your Renault dealer for the correct grade for your car.

Materials: Correct grade of brake fluid. Methylated spirits. Clean rag, free from fluff.

1 Before unscrewing the filler cap, clean the cap and the surrounding area to prevent grit or dirt falling into the reservoir. Use methylated spirits for cleaning as paraffin or mineral oil could contaminate the brake fluid.

2 Top-up the fluid to within ¼ in. (6 mm) below the threads of the filler cap. If the reservoir has 'Maxi' and 'Mini' or 'Danger' lines moulded on it, top-up to the 'Maxi' level. Never allow the fluid to fall below the minimum or danger marks.

3 Clean the inside of the filler cap and check that the air vent hole is not clogged.

4 If the fluid level has fallen noticeably, ask an assistant to depress the brake pedal firmly while you check all the unions and pipelines for any signs of leakage.

15.2 Changing the brake fluid

Brake fluid (and particularly the disc-brake type) absorbs moisture from the air through the vent hole in the reservoir filler cap. Some moisture slowly seeps through the flexible hoses and can also be drawn in past the wheel-cylinder seals. Since this moisture seriously lowers the boiling point of the fluid, 'vapour lock', which can cause complete brake failure, can result when the fluid boils in the wheel cylinders under heavy or prolonged braking conditions. The diagnosis is confirmed if normal braking is restored when the brakes cool down. The water in the fluid also corrodes the internal parts of the hydraulic components. The fluid should therefore be changed after 24 000 miles, or two years, in service. Some authorities recommend a yearly change of fluid.

Obviously, fluid should never be stored in an unsealed container. The old fluid that has been bled from the system must not be re-used.

Materials and tools: As for bleeding the brakes – see Section 15.3. About ½ litre (¾ pint) of fluid will be needed and this should leave some fluid over for subsequent topping-up.

The fluid is changed by opening the bleed screw on each wheel cylinder in turn, fitting a tube to the nipple, with its lower end in a suitable container, and pumping the brake pedal to expel the old fluid. The process is the same as for bleeding the brakes (Section 15.3) but all the old fluid in the system is pumped out and replaced by new fluid.

15.3 Bleeding the brakes

This is *not* a routine job. It should be necessary to expel air from the system only if any of the unions have been undone or new parts have been fitted, but air can be drawn in past worn wheel-cylinder or master-cylinder seals – in which case renewal of the parts is obviously indicated.

The brake-bleeding procedure is the same as for changing the fluid, but it is necessary only to pump the pedal until air bubbles no longer issue from the bleed pipe. The reservoir must be topped-up at frequent intervals to prevent air entering the system.

A nipple that incorporates a valve (and which ought to be fitted with a rubber dust cover) will be found on each caliper and backplate, next to the pipeline union. You will need the help of an assistant to do the job properly if any easy-bleeding device is not used.

To bleed the system –

Materials: Tin of correct grade of brake fluid (see Chapter 17).

Tools: Brake bleed valve spanner. Length of rubber or plastic tube to fit bleed nipple. Container for fluid bled from system. There are also a number of 'easy-bleeding' devices, obtainable from accessory shops, which make brake-bleeding a simple, one-man operation. Axle stand or support block for rear wheel – see above.

1 Attach a rubber or transparent plastic tube to the nipple on the wheel furthest from the master cylinder. Pass the tube through a box or ring spanner that fits the hexagon on the nipple. Submerge the free end of the tube in a little brake fluid in a clean glass jar.

2 Open the bleed screw one complete turn. Your assistant should now depress the brake pedal with a slow, full stroke and then allow it to return unassisted. Top-up the fluid level in the master cylinder reservoir with the fresh fluid. Repeat the pumping strokes after about 5 seconds.

3 Watch the flow of liquid into the jar and continue pumping until air bubbles cease. Tighten the bleed screw while the pedal is held down fully. *Do not over-tighten the screw.*

4 Repeat this operation on the other brakes, ending with the nipple nearest the master cylinder.

15.4 Brake adjustment – rear brakes only

If self-adjusting rear brakes are not fitted, two square adjusting spindles project from the backplate of each rear brake. The adjuster spindles are prone to seize-up and their flats can be quickly ruined by attempting to turn them with an unsuitable spanner. A special brake-adjusting spanner can be obtained quite cheaply from Halfords and other accessory shops.

To carry out the adjustment –

Tools: Jack. Axle stand. Brake-adjusting spanner.

1 Jack-up and support the wheel on which the brake is to be adjusted. The front wheels must be securely chocked and the handbrake released.

2 Turn the adjusters outwards from the centre of the wheel as shown in Fig. 15.3, beginning with the leading-shoe adjuster, which is in front of the axle on each brake.

3 Since the brake drums usually warp slightly in service, it may be necessary to accept slight rubbing at one or more points during rotation. Otherwise the adjuster would have to be slackened off to such an extent, before the drum was completely free, that excessive travel of the brake pedal would reduce braking efficiency.

4 Spin the wheel, apply the brakes hard and recheck the adjustment.

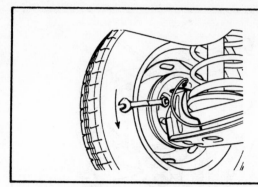

Fig. 15.3 Each drum brake has two adjusting spindles (one is shown). Turning the spanner outwards and downwards on each spindle takes up the clearance.

15.5 Handbrake cable adjustment

Normally, manual or automatic adjustment of the rear brake shoes will eliminate any excessive free movement on the handbrake lever. In time, however, the handbrake cable will stretch and it will be necessary to take up the slack by shortening the cable. When self-adjusting rear drum brakes are fitted the handbrake must never be adjusted during service. Adjustment should be needed only after a brake overhaul has been carried out.

To adjust the handbrake when manually-adjusted rear brakes are fitted –

Tools: Spanners. Jack. Axle stands.

1 Chock the front wheels securely and jack-up and support the rear of the car.

2 Release the handbrake and unlock the nuts 1 and 3 on the handbrake cable adjuster shown in Fig. 15.4.

3 Tighten the adjusting nut A, until the linings *just touch* the drum. Then slacken off slightly and make sure that the brakes are not binding.

4 Tighten the lock-nut.

To adjust the handbrake when self-adjusting rear brakes are fitted –

Since the action of the automatic adjusters can be upset by incorrect adjustment of the handbrake cable, this should not be disturbed unless a brake overhaul has been carried out or a cable has been renewed.

Tools: Spanners. Suitable method of lifting the car – see below.

1 The vehicle must be standing with all four wheels on the ground, or securely supported on suitable blocks if a hydraulic lift is not available.

2 Make sure that the handbrake lever is fully released and screw up the nut shown in Fig. 15.4 until the secondary cable is neither slack nor tight.

3 Check that the centre of the cable can be pulled down by a distance of about 20 mm (¾ in.). If the cable is

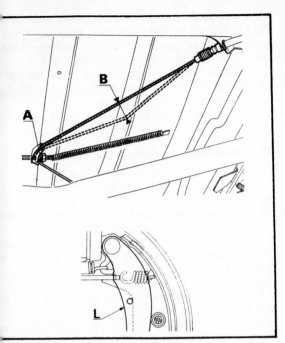

Fig. 15.4 Handbrake cable adjustment is carried out by rotating the nut A after slackening the lock-nut. When self-adjusting rear brakes are fitted the cable must be sufficiently slack to allow it to be pulled down below the floor at B to the extent of 20 mm. If the cable is too tight the lever L will become detached from the sector and the automatic adjuster will not function.

tighter than this, the self-adjuster lever will become detached from the toothed sector and the automatic adjustment will be put out of action.

4 To check that the tension is correct, pull up the handbrake. The travel should be between 12 and 13 notches.

15.6 Servicing manually-adjusted rear brakes

Dismantling drum brakes is quite straightforward, but a special Renault three-legged puller (tool No. T.Av.235) must normally be used to remove the brake drum. It may be possible to hire this tool from a Renault dealer, and this is always preferable to the use of improvised methods.

When the correct tool is not available, however, there are two alternative methods of withdrawing the drums which may be tried and which are described in the instructions which follow.

If grease has leaked from the hub bearings on to the brake shoes the oil seal in the hub must be renewed.

It is seldom advisable to clean grease-soaked linings with petrol or paraffin. It is also false economy to purchase cheap linings from a cut-price supplier, or to attempt to rivet new linings to the existing shoes, unless an efficient lining clamp is used. The safest plan is to fit factory-relined shoes.

If the brake drums are badly scored, have them reground or fit new drums.

It is always advisable to renew the pull-off springs when fitting replacement shoes. Weak springs can cause brake judder or squeal.

Clean out all the brake dust *but be careful not to inhale the dust, which contains asbestos and can harm the lungs.*

Materials: Paraffin. Methylated spirits. Penetrating oil or rust-releasing fluid. Clean rags. Anti-seize lubricant. High-temperature brake grease. Split-pin. For a complete overhaul: Replacement relined brake shoes. Set of new pull-off springs. Possibly, new wheel cylinders.

Tools: Brake adjusting spanner. Screwdriver. Pliers. Hammer, preferably copper- or hide-faced. Steel lever or strong screwdriver. Special tools: T.Av 235 (see above). Rou.441 (see item 2).

1 Jack-up the car and remove the wheel. Make sure that the handbrake is fully off and slacken back the adjusters so that the shoes are completely clear of the drum.

2 Remove the grease cap from the hub. Renault dealers use a special tool, Rou.441, but the cap can be removed by tapping it out with a wooden or brass drift, being careful not to dent it.

3 Remove the split-pin and the nut locking-plate and unscrew the nut from the end of the stub axle. Take off the washer.

4 Draw off the drum by using the special Renault tool shown in Fig. 15.5, or if this is not available, refit the road wheel and try to remove the drum by pulling on a wheel while rocking it in a horizontal and vertical direction in order to free the hub from the stub axle. Make sure that the car is really securely supported before doing this.

If this method is not successful, some owners use the wheel as an extractor by placing a suitably shaped piece of wood between the centre of the wheel and the end of the stub axle, the thickness of the distance-piece being chosen so that it is just possible to screw the wheel nuts on to the outer threads of the studs. By tightening each nut a little in rotation, it should be possible to pull off the drum. Excessive force must not be used, of course, owing to the risk of distorting the wheel.

5 Disconnect the handbrake cable from the lever. One end of the brake shoe retracting spring must now be disconnected from the shoe. Again a Renault dealer uses a special tool, but a tool can be made from a length of rod with a hooked end to engage with the end of the spring and pull it clear. An alternative method is to lever the tip of one shoe away from the brake expander, allowing the shoes to be collapsed together and the spring to be disengaged.

6 Remove the clips from behind the shoes and pull the shoes outwards, disengage the strut which is fitted between them and remove the shoes. Make a note of how everything fits together to ensure correct reas-

sembly. Preferably, deal with only one brake at a time, so that the other remains fully assembled and can be used as a reference.

7 Tie a length of string around the ends of the brake cylinder to prevent the piston creeping outwards, resulting in loss of fluid and entry of air into the system. Renault dealers use the wire clip shown in Fig. 15.6 but this is not essential.

8 Reassemble the brake mechanism. Smear the bearings with a little clean grease and tap the drum into place. Fit the washer and the axle nut and tighten the nut firmly while rotating the drum. The torque specified is 22 lb ft (30 Nm) and if possible a torque wrench should be used to obtain the correct load on the bearings.

9 Unscrew the hub nut by one quarter of a turn and pull the drum outwards so that it makes contact with the washer beneath the nut, either by using the Renault extractor, or by refitting the wheel and tugging it outwards, afterwards removing the wheel.

10 It should now be possible to feel a slight end-play on the bearings when the drum is pushed and pulled. A Renault dealer checks this with a dial gauge mounted on a bracket which is bolted to one of the wheel studs. The correct play is between 0.001–0.002 in. (0.01–0.05 mm). However, slackening back the hub nut by a quar-

ter of a turn will usually provide the correct end-float of the bearings. As a safety precaution, however, it might be as well to have your Renault dealer check the float of both hubs when the job has been completed.

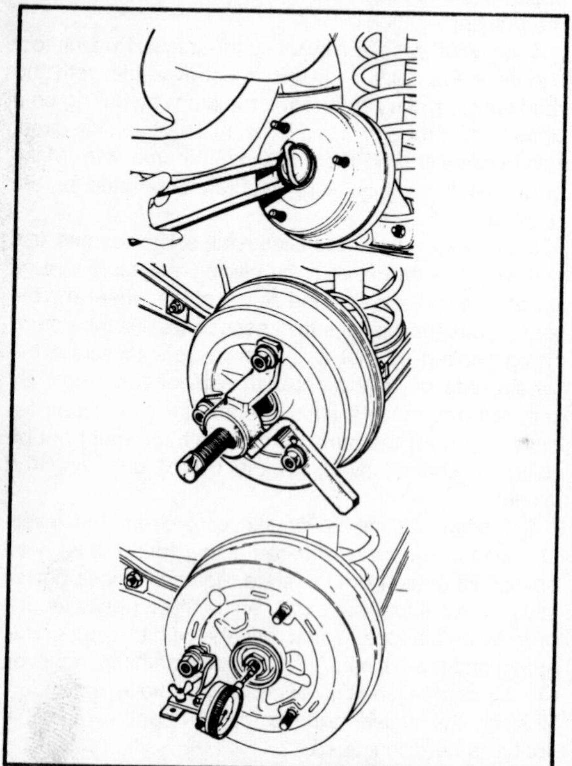

11 Fit the nut locking-plate and use a *new* split pin to lock the nut. Pack the grease cup three-quarters full of grease and tap it back into place.

12 Adjust the brake shoes as described in Section 15.4.

15.7 Servicing self-adjusting rear brakes

These brakes differ from the manually-adjusted type in having an adjusting lever and toothed sector fitted to the backplate. As will be seen from Fig. 15.8, the link which is fitted between the ends of the shoes is held in position by a spring which pulls on the trailing shoe. When the wheel cylinder pushes the shoes outwards the link moves with the trailing shoe and at the same time pulls the adjusting lever and the toothed sector towards the centre of the backplate.

If the minimum clearance exists between the shoes and the drum, the teeth on the lever and the sector remain in mesh, but if excessive clearance exists the teeth on the lever disengage from those on the sector and under the influence of the spring the sector moves back to the extent of one tooth on the lever.

When the shoes retract they cannot now return to their original position since the link, pressing both on the shoes and the adjusting lever, will hold them apart to give the correct shoe-to-drum clearance.

When servicing self-adjusting rear brakes the sequence is virtually the same as for manually-adjusted brakes as described in Section 15.6 but the following points should be borne in mind –

Materials and tools: as for Section 15.6.

1 Before the drum can be removed it is advisable to zero the adjustment – otherwise the shoes may catch

Fig. 15.5 Renault dealers use the three tools shown when removing and refitting a brake drum. Top, hub-cap removal tool. Centre, brake-drum extractor. Bottom, dial gauge and bracket, used to measure the end-float on the hub bearing.

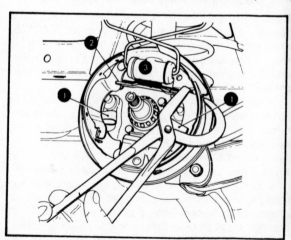

Fig. 15.6 A drum brake with the drum removed. 1, shoe clips. 2, strut, with pull-off spring above it. 3, brake cylinder (with wire clamp fitted to prevent pistons expanding during dismantling). The special spring-removing tool shown is not essential.

gainst the ridge formed by the unworn section of the drum. On earlier models there is a hole in the drum, sealed by a plug, through which a 3/16 in. (5 mm) diameter rod can be inserted as shown in Fig. 15.9. The rod should rest against the toothed sector and the drum should be turned in a forward direction to disengage the sector from the base of the adjusting lever. Incidentally only the later type of drum, without an access hole (see item 2 below) is supplied as a spare. If one of these drums is to be fitted to an earlier brake an access hole must be drilled as shown in Fig. 15.10.

2 The later pattern of brake has the access hole in the backplate instead of in the drum. Remove the sealing plug and insert a screwdriver so that it rests on the handbrake lever and push the lever to free the peg shown in Fig. 15.10 from the brake lever. Then push the lever to the rear to assist it to back-off.

3 When the drum has been removed the shoes can be taken off by removing the top pull-off spring, disconnecting the handbrake cable and unhooking the steady springs from the webs of the shoes. Then push the adjusting lever over towards the stub axle as far as possible and ease the shoes away from the backplate. Pull the link outwards and disengage the leading shoe from it. Set the toothed sector in its initial position, tilt the leading shoe outwards and remove the bottom return spring. Both shoes can then be removed.

4 When refitting the shoes, carry out the sequence in reverse. Insert the steady spring attachments in their locations in the backplate and rotate them through a quarter-turn.

5 Check the adjustment of the self-adjusting mechanism by measuring the gap between the end of the link and the edge of the slot in the shoe as shown in Fig. 15.15. This should be 1 mm (3/64 in.). If the gap is incorrect, the tension spring between the shoe and the other end of the link must be renewed, together with both shoe return springs.

6 When the brake drum has been refitted press the brake pedal to restore the correct clearance and then adjust the handbrake cable, if necessary – see Section 15.15.

15.8 Fitting new friction pads to disc brakes

Fitting replacement pads to the front disc brakes is quite straightforward although, unlike the case with the majority of British cars, it is necessary to remove the calipers in order to change the pads. All the brake pads on the pair of brakes on one axle must be changed together, and the pads of different makes and different grades must never be mixed.

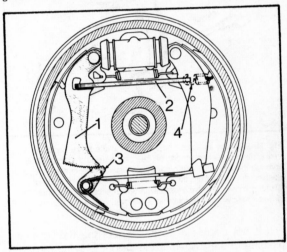

Fig. 15.8 A self-adjusting rear brake. The parts shown are: 1, adjusting lever. 2, link. 3, toothed quadrant. 4, coil spring. 5, quadrant return spring.

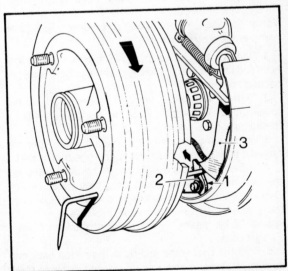

Fig. 15.9 'Zeroing' the self adjuster when an access hole is drilled in the brake drum. A rod is inserted to move the quadrant 1 against the tension of the spring 2 by rotating the brake drum, thus freeing the adjusting lever 3.

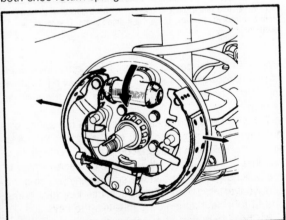

Fig. 15.7 When the spring has been removed, the shoes can be pulled outwards to disengage them. The hydraulic cylinder can be pulled downwards and outwards after disconnecting the fluid pipe and the retainer on the backplate.

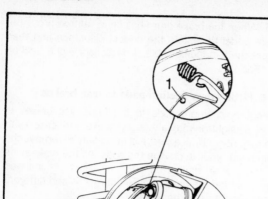

Fig. 15.10 When an access hole is drilled in the brake backplate the self-adjusting mechanism can be freed by passing the screwdriver through the backplate and through a clearance hole in the shoe, and pushing the peg 1 from the shoe. When a later pattern of drum is fitted to an earlier brake assembly, a 5 mm access hole 2 must be drilled as shown, the distance at 3 being 85 mm — see Section 15.7.

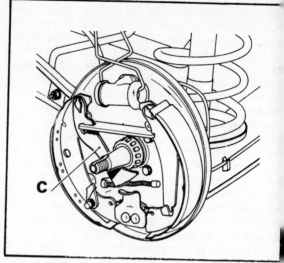

Fig. 15.11 When removing self-adjusting shoes, tilt the toothed lever C as far as possible towards the stub axle and ease the shoes away from the backplate.

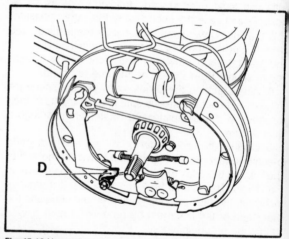

Fig. 15.12 Next pull the link between the shoes outwards to free it from the leading shoe and place the toothed sector D in its initial position.

It is not necessary to disconnect the flexible brake pipes from the calipers if the caliper is being removed only to change the pads.

Materials: New set of pads and spring clips. Disc-brake piston grease. Methylated spirits. Paint brush. Cloth. Small block of wood.

Tools: Spanners. Pliers. Strong screwdriver. Soft-faced hammer. Lever. Pin punch.

1 Remove the spring clips which retain the caliper keys and tap out one of the keys with a punch. Slide the second key out.

2 Remove the caliper. While it is detached, do not touch the brake pedal; otherwise the pistons will be forced out of the caliper.

3 Remove the pads from the sides of the caliper and take out the springs which are fitted beneath the pads.

4 Remove the dust cover from its housing and clean the end of the piston, using only methylated spirits. Other solvents, such as petrol or paraffin, will damage the piston seal. Lubricate the side of the piston with special brake grease, which can be obtained from a Renault dealer.

5 Refit the dust cover and push the piston back into its cylinder, using a new pad, a wooden distance block and a screwdriver as a lever.

6 Refit the springs beneath the pads, followed by the pads themselves. When the springs are of unequal length, fit the longest on the outside. Some later types of pad differ from this earlier pattern in having a retaining stop. These pads must be fitted with the stop as shown in Fig. 15.19.

7 Fit one end of the caliper between the spring clip and the keyway on the caliper bracket. Place the other end of the caliper in position, compressing both springs, and insert the first key. Place the tip of a screwdriver in the second keyway and fit the second key by using the screwdriver as a lever. Finally tap this key fully home and fit four new spring clips to retain the keys.

8 Check with the other caliper assembly, which has not been dismantled, to make sure that everything is correctly assembled. Press the brake pedal several times to bring the pistons into contact with the pads.

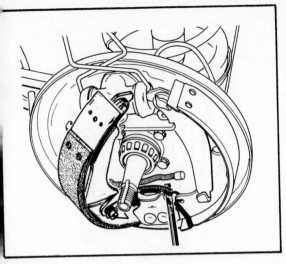

Fig. 15.13 Finally tilt the leading shoe through 90°, and disengage the bottom return spring, allowing the leading and trailing shoes to be removed.

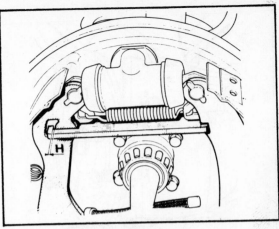

Fig. 15.15 Measure the distance H between the link and the leading shoe when the brake has been assembled. It should be 1 mm.

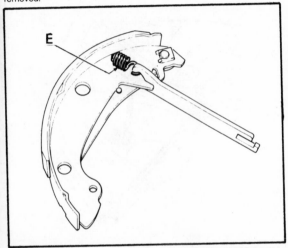

Fig. 15.14 When reassembling a self-adjusting brake, make sure that the spring E is correctly hooked between the link and the trailing shoe.

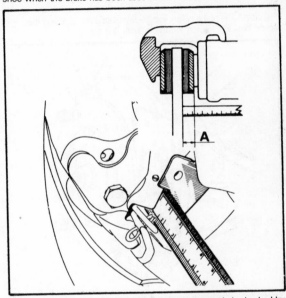

Fig. 15.16 The thickness of the front brake friction pads is checked by measuring the depth of the complete pad, as shown. The measurement at A should not be less than 7 mm (about ¼ in.).

15.9 The rear-brake pressure limiting valve

The maximum pressure in the rear brake operating cylinders is controlled by a pressure-limiting valve. This is attached to a bracket on the underside of the car and coupled to the upper rear suspension arm by a lever and an adjustable rod.

The valve controls the rear brake pressure in proportion to the amount of weight which is carried in the rear of the car, thus helping to prevent the rear wheels locking prematurely under heavy braking conditions. The heavier the load in the rear, the greater the adhesion between the rear tyres and the road – so under these conditions the valve allows a greater pressure to build up in the rear brake cylinders.

The limiting valve cannot be serviced. If it is thought to be faulty it must be renewed. First, however, have the adjustment at the end of the vertical threaded rod checked by a Renault dealer, who will have a special pressure gauge, capable of reading to over 600 lb/sq in., which can be connected to one of the rear brake cylinders by a union which replaces the bleed screw.

The correct cut-off pressure varies quite considerably to the particular model and the amount of petrol in the tank and in view of the vital safety aspect of this adjustment it is essential to let your Renault dealer carry it out.

If the vertical rod must be disconnected at any time, do not alter the position of the two adjusting nuts on it as these regulate the pressure transmitted to the rear wheel cylinders. If the top nut is slackened off and the

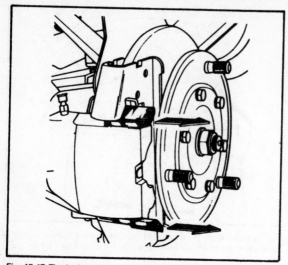

Fig. 15.17 The brake caliper can be removed after removing the spring clips and tapping out the retaining keys.

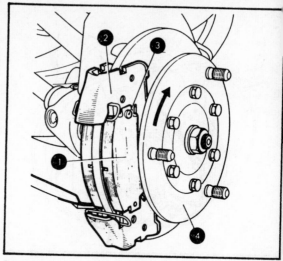

Fig. 15.19 Some later pads, which are fitted with a peg, must be positioned as shown. 1, pad. 2, caliper. 3, locating peg. 4, wheel hub.

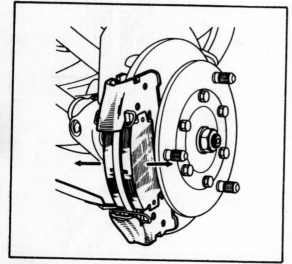

Fig. 15.18 With the caliper out of the way the pads can be withdrawn as shown.

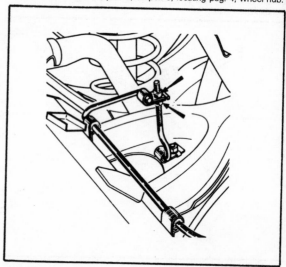

Fig. 15.20 The rear-brake pressure limiting valve is controlled by the lever and the adjustable rod shown. The adjustment of the nuts indicated by the arrows should not be disturbed, as special equipment is needed to reset the valve.

bottom nut is screwed up, the pressure will be increased. Conversely, slackening off the bottom nut and screwing the top nut downwards will reduce the pressure.

15.10 The brake pressure-drop indicator

When a tandem master cylinder is used in conjunction with split braking circuits, a pressure-drop indicator may be fitted. This operates only when the balance of the pressure in the pipelines is upset for some reason – for example if the system requires bleeding, or if there is an external leak of fluid, or an operating fault in the tandem master cylinder.

The indicator unit contains two small pistons which normally take up a central position. If an unbalanced

pressure develops, the pistons may move away from the centre of the bore and operate the plunger of a switch which controls a warning lamp on the instrument panel.

The indicator unit cannot be repaired. It is mounted beside the master cylinder and if it is necessary to change it the replacement must be lined-up at an angle of about 30° in relation to the horizontal centre-line of the master cylinder, as shown in Fig. 15.21. After reconnecting the pipelines as illustrated and the switch wire, bleed the system as described in Section 15.3.

15.11 The pressure-drop bypass unit

A pressure-drop indicator bypass unit may be provided on

cars for some markets. This operates in a similar manner to the pressure-drop indicator described in the previous section but has the added function of increasing the pressure to the rear brakes if a leak should occur in the front-brake hydraulic circuit.

What has been said concerning the normal pressure-drop indicator applies also to this unit but the additional hydraulic circuit served by the unit must be bled after the four wheel cylinders have been bled as described in Section 15.3. A bleed valve is fitted on the upper side of the unit.

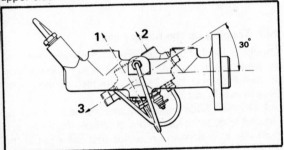

Fig. 15.21 When a pressure-drop indicator is fitted, it must be inclined at an angle of 30° to the master-cylinder axis as shown. 1 is the outlet to the right-hand front wheel, 2 the outlet to the rear wheels and 3 the outlet to the left-hand front wheel.

The vacuum servo

When a servo is provided it is mounted in the engine compartment. It requires no attention, except to renew the air filter after about 18 000 miles in service – see below.

If the servo does not operate, first check that there is no leakage at the unions in the hose connecting it to the inlet manifold, and that the hose itself is not perished or collapsed. If all seems to be in order here, ask your dealer to vet the servo. If the trouble is more than a trivial fault a new servo must be fitted, since this unit is not repairable.

Should the servo fail for any reason, fluid can still flow through it to the brakes, but a considerably heavier pressure on the brake pedal will be required to obtain the same braking power.

15.12 Cleaning or renewing the servo air filter

It is not necessary to remove the servo from the car in order to change the air filter.

Tools: Spanners. Pliers. Scriber or other sharp-pointed tool. Rule.

1 Remove the pin from the fork which connects the servo operating rod to the brake pedal.

2 Measure the distance from the flat face of the servo to the outer end of the fork.

3 Unscrew the lock-nut and screw the fork-end off the servo rod. Remove the retaining spring and extract the air filter with a sharp-pointed tool.

4 Fit the new filter and the retainer.

5 Screw the locking nut and the fork-end on to the shaft and adjust the fork to give the dimension previously measured. This controls the position of the brake pedal.

6 Refit the pin in the fork.

15.13 Changing the servo one-way valve

If this valve, which maintains the vacuum in the servo, is faulty, the servo will operate only when the engine is running.

To change the valve –

1 Disconnect the vacuum pipe from the brake servo.

2 Pull out the valve, turning it at the same time to free it from the rubber sealing washer.

3 Check the condition of the sealing washer and fit the new valve.

4 Reconnect the vacuum servo pipe.

16 The electrical system

Routine servicing of the electrical system is quite straightforward, calling for no specialized equipment; nor should simple fault-tracing and first-aid measures present any problems. If any serious troubles crop up, however, it is best to take advantage of the service-exchange scheme operated by your dealer, under which a faulty component is replaced by a reconditioned, guaranteed unit at a fixed charge (this subject is discussed in more detail in Chapter 8).

The time factor

The maintenance checks and simple servicing work described in this chapter do not normally call for pre-planning, minor jobs taking only a few minutes each. Suggested times for more ambitious work are: Removing and refitting the alternator, 45 min; removing and refitting the starter motor, 45-60 min; overhauling a starter motor, 2 hr.

16.1 Battery maintenance

An excellent safety feature is that in the event of a short-circuit occurring, the battery can be instantly disconnected by unscrewing the knob on the negative battery post by a few turns, but never do this when the engine is running, as it will damage the alternator.

The tops of the cells must be kept clean and dry, to prevent corrosion of the terminals and leakage of current.

The battery-retaining clamp should be just sufficiently tight to prevent movement of the battery on its mounting. Overtightening it may crack or distort the battery case.

To clean the terminals and terminal posts —
1 Take off the connectors.
2 Scrape any corrosion off the terminals.
3 Replace the connectors and tighten the retaining screws. Smear the terminals and posts with petroleum jelly to protect them against corrosion.
4 Don't overlook the connections at the earthed end of the battery earthing strap, at the starter motor and at the solenoid switch. These connections must be clean and secure.

16.2 Topping up the battery cells

Check the level of the liquid (the electrolyte) in each cell at weekly intervals and don't allow it to fall lower than 15 mm (just over ½ in.) above the tops of the plates. Bear in mind the following points —

1 Distilled, demineralized or 'purified' water is obtainable quite cheaply from chemists. Tapwater and rainwater may contain impurities that will shorten the life of the battery. In an emergency, water from the drip-tray of a refrigerator which has been defrosted can be used, but not the water obtained by melting ice cubes.

2 Never use a naked flame when inspecting the fluid level or allow sparking to occur near the battery when it is being charged. A mixture of hydrogen and oxygen is produced when the electrolyte begins to bubble and if this is ignited the battery can explode.

3 Add water just before the cells are to be charged, to allow the acid and water to mix thoroughly, and to avoid any risk of the water freezing, expanding and damaging the plates and battery case in cold weather.

4 The need for frequent topping-up usually suggests too high a generator charging rate. If one cell regularly requires more than the others, it is probably leaking. Unless the battery is nearly new, or still under guarantee, repairs to individual cells are not usually worthwhile.

5 It should not be necessary to add *acid* to the cells unless some of the electrolyte has been spilt, in which case it would be wise to have a word with your dealer.

6 Finally, remember that the electrolyte is a very corrosive solution of sulphuric acid in water. If any is spilled, wipe it away immediately with a clean wet cloth and then dry the part thoroughly. Household ammonia will neutralize the acid.

16.3 Battery charge indicator

The battery charge indicator on the instrument panel shows whether the battery is receiving an adequate charge from the alternator, and also whether it is well charged. The indicator is a voltmeter, operated by a bi-metal spring — not an ammeter which records the current passing to the battery.

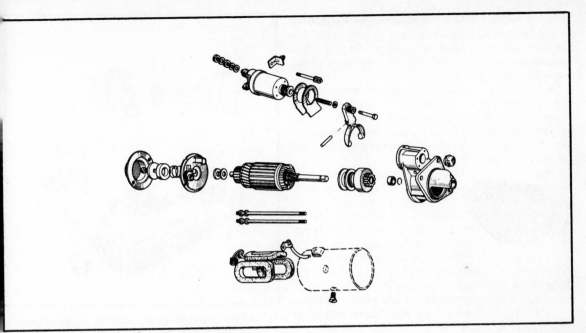

Fig. 16.1 A typical Ducellier starter completely dismantled.

When the charging rate is low, or the battery is discharged, the voltage will be low and the needle will be towards the left-hand end of the scale. With a well-charged battery and a normal charging rate the needle will be in the central sector. It may drop into the low sector immediately after switching on a fairly heavy load, such as the headlamps or a heated rear window, but should quickly stabilize.

If the needle consistently reads low, or if it is constantly in the high sector, have the alternator and the regulator checked by a Renault dealer or an auto-electrician. If you have a voltmeter, however, first make the checks described in Section 16.17.

16.4 Servicing an alternator

An alternator requires no routine maintenance, except for keeping the terminals clean and the end-plate free from deposits of dust and grease and checking the driving belt tension as described in Chapter 10. There are, however, several practical points to be remembered when dealing with an alternator which may be overlooked by an owner who has previously dealt only with dynamos.

If the battery has been removed, when refitting it, first connect the negative battery terminal to the earth strap and then fit the positive terminal connector. *Never disconnect the battery when the engine is running.*

Care must be taken not to earth the regulator or the 'EXC' wire on the alternator. Never run the engine with the main output cable from the alternator disconnected.

If a charger is to be used to charge-up a flat battery, first isolate the alternator by disconnecting both battery terminals.

If the charging circuit gives trouble, or the alternator requires routine servicing, the work should always be done by a fully-qualified auto-electrician.

16.5 Starter motor servicing

The models covered by this book are fitted with Paris-Rhône or Ducellier pre-engaged starter motors. In these starters the pinion is moved into engagement with the flywheel ring by a solenoid-operated lever, before the pinion starts to rotate.

The starter should be serviced at reasonable intervals – say, every 36 000 miles – when it should be removed from the car as described in Section 16.6 and dismantled so that the commutator, brushes and the pinion-drive components can be inspected and cleaned.

If the starter is to be completely dismantled, the exploded views in Figs. 16.1 and 16.2 will clearly show the relationship of the various parts. Stripping is straightforward, but note the following points –

Materials: New brushes and drive parts, as needed. Paraffin. Clean cloth. Solder and flux.
Tools: Screwdriver. Pliers. Hammer. Soldering iron. Feeler gauges. Pin punch.

1 The pin on which the solenoid operating fork pivots may be retained by a spring clip at one end. If a plain pin is fitted it must be tapped out by applying a pin-punch to its left-hand end, as viewed from the pinion end of the assembly, to avoid damaging the fork bearing. When refitting the pin, tap it in from the right-hand side.

2 If the commutator is blackened or scored, take the armature and commutator assembly to a Renault dealer for reconditioning. Light scoring can be cleaned off with

fine emery cloth, followed by cleaning-out the grooves in the commutator and a final clean-up with petrol. The brushes can be renewed by taking off the end cover, unsoldering the leads and soldering the leads of the new brushes to the connectors.

3 The various washers on the armature must be fitted correctly. With a Ducellier starter, the steel washer goes on first, followed by the fibre washer. After greasing the rear bush and fitting the body and the rear bearing, fit the spring washer and then the plastic washer, noting the position of the slots.

The arrangement of the plain steel washers, wave washers and the fibre washer on a Paris-Rhône starter is shown in Fig. 16.3.

4 When refitting the solenoid to a Ducellier starter, first screw in the bolt which passes through the upper end of the fork and tighten it fully while holding the armature core. Then check the adjustment of the solenoid and fork assembly by removing the plug from the front of the solenoid and checking that there is only a very slight clearance between the bolt and the adjusting nut at F in Fig. 16.5, when the pinion assembly is resting against the armature. Next push the solenoid bolt inwards and check that a clearance of 0.002-0.06 in. (0.05-1.5 mm) exists between the outer face of the pinion and the collar on the shaft, at G in Fig. 16.5. If necessary turn the adjusting nut on the end of the solenoid to obtain the correct clearance at F and G.

16.6 Removing and refitting the starter motor

Tools: Spanners. Screwdriver. Pliers.

1 Disconnect the battery by unscrewing the wing-nut on the positive terminal. Then disconnect the positive lead from the starter motor and the feed wire from the solenoid.

2 Remove the air filter and the starter heat shield.

3 Unscrew the starter retaining bolts and remove the starter by turning it sideways and lifting it out towards the front.

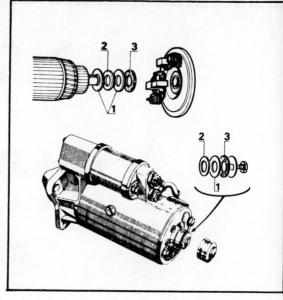

Fig. 16.3 The correct assembly of the washers on a Paris-Rhône starter armature shaft. 1, steel washer. 2, wave washer. 3, fibre washer.

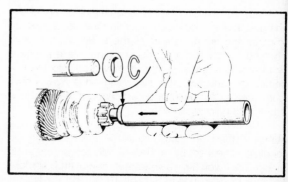

Fig. 16.4 To remove the drive pinion the snap ring must be released by tapping it with a piece of tube. When reassembling fit the snap ring first and then push the stop back over it.

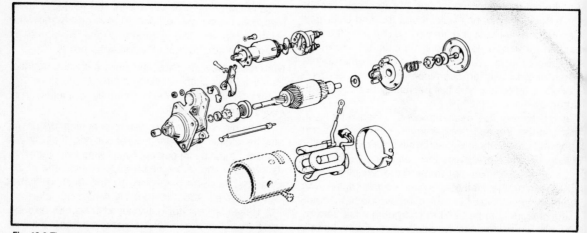

Fig. 16.2 The component parts of a typical Paris-Rhône starter motor.

Although the bulbs are prefocused and the design of the holders should ensure correct location, it is always advisable to have the beam alignment checked as described in Section 16.9 after a new bulb has been fitted.

To change a tungsten-filament bulb (used for both main and dipped beams in all models except the later TS which has quartz-iodine bulbs for the main beams) –

Tools: Screwdriver.

1 Remove the headlamp rim, which is retained by screws at the top and by lugs at the bottom. Open the bonnet, take out the screws and pull the top of the rim upwards and outwards to disengage the lugs.

2 Push the spring clip at one upper corner of the reflector and lens unit aside and then swing the unit outwards from the top and unhook the lower retaining lug.

3 Pull off the connector, unclip the springs which secure the bulb and remove the bulb. If a new bulb is being fitted, remove the sealing washer from the old bulb, fit it to the new one and fit the bulb so that the projection on its flange locates correctly in the slot in the housing.

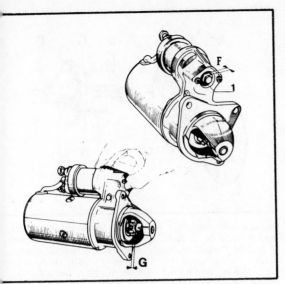

Fig. 16.5 When reassembling a Ducellier starter, the clearances at the points F and G must be correct. The method of carrying out the adjustment is described in Section 16.5.

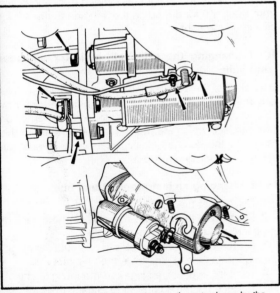

Fig. 16.6 When removing the starter motor the nuts shown by the arrows must be unscrewed and the starter withdrawn by moving it sideways and towards the front of the car.

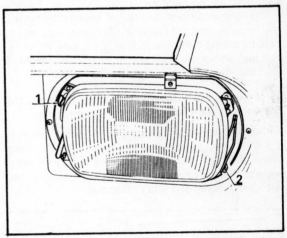

Fig. 16.7 When removing a headlamp the panel embellisher must be taken off to allow the clip 1 to be lifted and the light unit to be tilted forward to free the hook 2.

16.7 Removing and refitting a headlamp unit or bulb

When fitting a headlamp bulb be careful not to touch the glass with the fingers, as the slightest trace of grease or moisture will be carbonized by the heat of the filament, reducing the amount of light emitted by the bulb. This is particularly important with halogen headlamps, in which the bulbs run at a very high temperature. Handle the bulb only with a tissue or a clean dry cloth.

To change a quartz-iodine bulb –

Tools: Screwdriver.

1 First remove the light unit as described above and then disconnect the central connector from the rear of the light unit and the second connector for the wires which emerge from the side of the light unit.

2 Pull the rubber cover away and disconnect the spade terminal from the bulb holder.

3 The quartz-iodine bulb is retained by a spring which rests in a slot. Press the spring firmly to release it and withdraw the bulb.

16.8 Headlamp beam adjustment – load setting

The headlamp beams can be raised or lowered to suit the load carried by the car, either by moving a small lever which projects beside each headlamp lens, or when adjustment can be carried out from the driving compartment, by turning a knob on the fascia panel. Raising the lever or turning the knob clockwise will lower the beams to compensate for the tail-down attitude when the car is fully laden, whereas lowering the lever or turning the knob anti-clockwise will raise the beams to their normal position.

16.9 Headlamp beam alignment checks

In addition to the adjustments described in Sections 16.8 and 16.10, the reflectors must be pre-set by means of adjusting screws to ensure that the beams will be correctly aligned, both as regards their height and direction.

It is difficult to carry out this adjustment by hit-and-miss methods in the home garage. If the car is due for a MoT test, it is quite likely to be failed on this score if special beam-setting equipment has not been used. Most service stations, however, should be able to check, and if necessary adjust, the beam alignment with the aid of optical equipment.

The headlamp beam is raised or lowered by turning the screw A shown in Fig. 16.8 and swung from side to side by turning the screw B. First make sure, however, that the lever or the knob which controls the height of the beam is set in the normal raised position.

16.10 Headlamp beam adjustment for driving on the left-hand or right-hand side of the road

A further refinement which is provided on some models is a small setting lever at the rear of the reflector which allows the bulb holder to be rotated through a small angle to give the correct dipped beam for driving on the left-hand or right-hand side of the road.

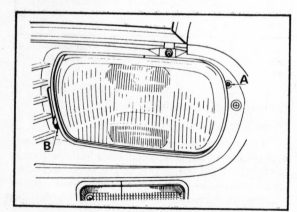

Fig. 16.8 Before aligning the headlamp beam, place the setting lever or the dashboard control in the normal position and then turn screw A to swing the beam from side to side, and the screw B to raise and lower it.

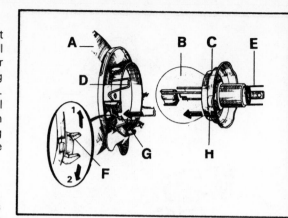

Fig. 16.9 Some headlights have a rotator which enables the dipped beam to be altered for driving on the left-hand or the right-hand side of the road. The parts shown are: A, light unit. B, bulb. C, stepped flange. D, clip. E, connector. F, small level (rotator). G, slot for bulb lug. H, bulb lug. With the bulb removed, move the lever in the direction of 1 for driving on the right or towards 2 for driving on the left.

Remove the bulb as described in Section 16.7 and move the lever to the right (as viewed from above and from the front) for driving on the left, and to the left for driving on the right.

16.11 Changing the side, tail, indicator and rear lamp bulbs

Inspection of the side, tail, indicator and rear lamp bulbs is quite straightforward, the covers being retained by screws except for the front indicator and side lamps on later models, which are housed in the bumper. In this case turn the serrated plastic bulb holder through an eighth of a turn to remove it.

16.12 Changing an instrument panel bulb

1 Disconnect the battery.
2 Disconnect the junction box blocks at the back of the panel and the speedometer cable.
3 Lift the two retaining clips and push the panel out, freeing the mounting lugs from their holders.
4 To refit the panel, engage the mounting lugs with their holders, push the panel in to engage the clips and reconnect the junction blocks and speedometer cable.

16.13 The windscreen wiper and washer

The wiper normally requires no attention, other than renewal of the wiper blades at least once a year.

If the blades do not sweep a clean arc, wash the rubbers and the screen with a special windscreen detergent such as Trico SR-12 to remove deposits of diesel fumes, which will cause persistent smearing. Always add a wiper-fluid detergent to the water in the washer reservoir, using an anti-freeze type in winter. Do not use ordinary radiator anti-freeze solution, which will damage the paintwork.

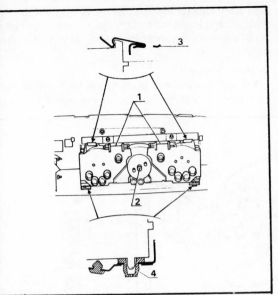

Fig. 16.10 To remove the instrument panel it is necessary to disconnect the junction blocks 1 and the speedometer cable 2 before lifting the retaining clips 3. The panel can then be pulled out, freeing the mounting lugs 4 from their holders.

16.14 Direction indicators

The flashing indicator lamps are fed with current from a sealed control unit. Failure or erratic action of the indicators may be caused by a blown bulb, dirty contacts in the indicator switch or in the lamp units, or by faulty wiring or a blown fuse. If checks on these points do not reveal any faults, the flasher unit is probably the culprit and must be replaced, since it is not repairable.

The flasher unit is held behind the fascia panel. When removing and refitting it label the leads to match the '+', 'Com' and 'Rep' terminals.

16.15 Testing a faulty brake stop-light switch

The switch is operated by the shank of the brake pedal, contact being made as soon as the pedal moves away from the plunger of the switch.

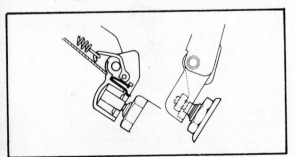

Fig. 16.11 The method of removing the wiper arms from their spindles depends on the design. With the earlier pattern shown on the left, lift the catch and pull off the arm. With the later pattern, lift the base of the arm to reveal the retaining nut and unscrew the nut.

To check the circuit –

1 If the stop lights flicker or do not come on when the brake pedal is depressed, check the lamp bulbs, holders, wiring and the fuse.

2 If everything seems to be in order, disconnect the wires from the stop-lamp switch, switch on the ignition and touch the terminals on the wires together. If the stop-lamps then light up, either the stop-lamp switch is faulty or the leads were making poor contact with the terminals on the switch. If the stop-lamps do not come on when the wires are short-circuited, there must be a fault at some point in the wiring or the fuse has blown (see Section 16.16).

16.16 The fuses

The number and position of the fuses varies with different models. There may be only two in a holder in the engine compartment mounted on the left-hand front wheel housing. On early models both these may be rated at 15-amp whereas on later cars there may be an 8-amp and a 5-amp fuse in this holder. The circuits which are protected can be checked by removing each fuse in turn, to discover which units – for example the instruments, stop-lamps, windscreen wiper, interior light, or the heater fan motor – become inoperative when the fuse is taken out.

On some earlier versions there is a fuse box under the dashboard which contains 8-amp fuses which protect the windscreen wiper and the headlamp main and dipped beams.

A heated rear window on earlier cars may be served by an 8-amp fuse in a bayonet-type fuse holder clipped to the right-hand side of the steering column, and the flasher unit by a 5-amp fuse in a similar holder on the left-hand side of the column.

The usual arrangement on later cars is to fit six fuses in a holder under the dashboard. Reading from the top downwards there is a 16-amp fuse for the instruments, stop-lights and heated rear window; a 5-amp fuse for the automatic transmission, when fitted; a 5-amp fuse for the direction indicators; an 8-amp fuse for the heater fan; an 8-amp fuse for the interior light and glove compartment; and an 8-amp fuse for the windscreen washer and wiper.

As has already been mentioned, however, different layouts may be found, so when replacing a burnt-out fuse first identify the circuits which have been put out of action and always fit a new fuse of the same rating as the original. Never be tempted to bridge the terminals with ordinary wire, as this could result in a component being burnt out or a fire being started in the wiring.

Simple fault-tracing

There are some simple tests that can be made when it is suspected that the generator is not giving its full charge.

16.17 Testing the generator and charging system

The following tests, for which only a voltmeter is required, are sufficient to show whether or not all is well with the alternator and the charging system. A moving-coil type of meter is to be preferred, but any good-quality instrument can be used, as the checks depend on comparative readings, rather than on exact voltages.

They are based on the fact that the battery voltage varies according to the state of charge and is always higher when the cells are receiving a charge from the alternator.

To make the test –

1 Clip the voltmeter leads to the battery terminals, making sure that the surface of the metal has been

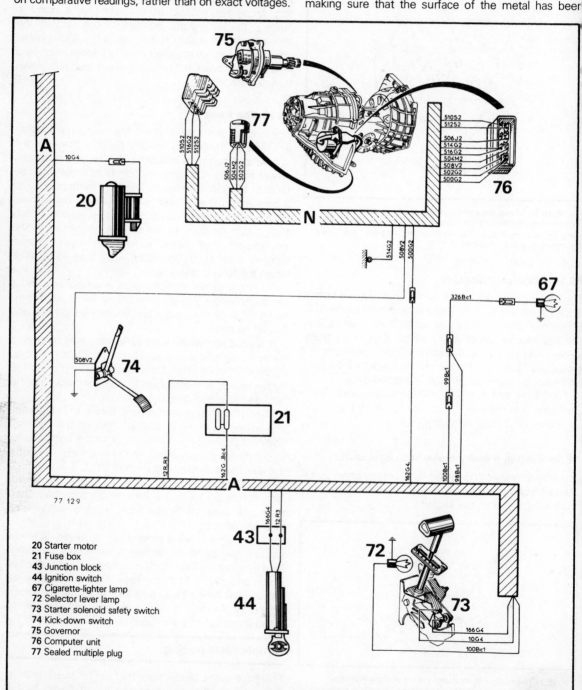

77 129

20 Starter motor
21 Fuse box
43 Junction block
44 Ignition switch
67 Cigarette-lighter lamp
72 Selector lever lamp
73 Starter solenoid safety switch
74 Kick-down switch
75 Governor
76 Computer unit
77 Sealed multiple plug

Fig. 16.12 A circuit diagram for the electrical controls and components of an automatic transmission.

pierced. If the battery is sound and well charged, a reading of 12–12.5 volts should be obtained.

2 Switch on all the lights. The reading should now fall to approximately 11–11.5 volts.

3 Start the engine and speed it up to the equivalent of about 20 mph in top gear, but do not race it. The reading should now be about 13.5 volts, and the voltmeter needle should be steady. If it flickers, there may be a bad contact in the wiring, the alternator commutator may be dirty, the brushes may be worn or sticking, or the regulator may be faulty.

4 If voltage readings roughly equal to those quoted are obtained, it can be assumed that the battery and charging system are sound. If the voltage across the battery does not rise by 1 volt when the engine is speeded-up above idling speed, there is a fault somewhere in the charging system, probably one of those just mentioned. If the increase exceeds about 1.5 volts, either the regulator is incorrectly adjusted or the battery is faulty. Do not try to adjust the regulator. Leave this sort of work to a qualified auto-electrician.

16.18 Wiring diagrams

The increasing tendency to separate the wiring looms of modern cars into convenient sections which are coupled together by junction blocks or by non-reversible multi-pin connectors makes life easier for the service engineer and, of course, for the practical owner who wants to replace a faulty section of the loom with the minimum cost and expenditure of time and effort.

When the insulation is damaged or a wire is burnt-out as a result of a short-circuit or a fault in a component, the adjacent wires in the loom are almost invariably damaged, so replacement of the affected section is the only practicable course.

Bearing this in mind, we have included in this chapter and on the back cover of this book, diagrams of the connectors for the components which are likely to be removed for servicing or repair. The colour-coding of the wires should prevent any possibility of incorrect connections, although this is often taken care of by the design of the connectors themselves.

17 Specifications and overhaul data

In this chapter we have included specifications and data which will be needed to carry out adjustments, overhauls and replacements which are within the scope of a d.i.y. owner.

We have avoided giving lists of fits, clearances and engineering tolerances which call for the use of micrometers and similar precision equipment, however, as these are not likely to be found – or needed – in the average home garage.

As we recommend in Chapter 8, highly skilled work of this sort should be left to a Renault dealer or to a specialist who is best qualified to handle it.

Alternatively, it is often possible to fit reconditioned components, the cost of which can show a considerable saving over the price of new parts.

Some parts are retained by self-locking nuts in which the locking effect is obtained by distorting the thread. If these nuts are removed they must be replaced by conventional self-locking nuts which have nylon inserts. Deformed-thread nuts are identified by two lines on one flat and a chamfer on the upper surface.

Top-up and fill-up data

Capacities (approx.)

Fuel tank: up to October 1975	11 gal (50 litres)
from October 1975 on	10¼ gal (47 litres)
Engine oil capacity	5¼ pints (3 litres)
(When the oil filter is changed, add an extra ½ pint, 0.25 litre)	
Cooling system	8¾ pints (5 litres)
Gearbox/differential: 12L, TL, TN up to October 1975	3 pints (1.7 litres)
12TS and all models after October 1975	3½ pints (2 litres)
Automatic transmission, including torque converter	9 pints (5 litres)
Quantity required for refilling after draining (depending on amount retained in torque converter)	5½–6½ pints (3–4 litres)

Recommended fuel grade

8.5:1 compression-ratio models – see page 105	3-star (94 octane, minimum)
9.5:1 compression-ratio models – see page 105	4-star (97 octane, minimum)

It is important to use a fuel that has a sufficiently high octane rating to prevent detonation ('pinking') under load, which can cause overheating and may damage the pistons and engine bearings.

Oil consumption

A reasonable consumption for a *worn* engine is about 500–750 miles per pint. The figure for a new or reconditioned engine may be as high as 350 miles per pint, gradually improving during the first 2000–3000 miles as the piston rings and cylinder walls bed-in, and eventually becoming negligible between oil changes.

Recommended lubricants (temperate climates)

Engine	Multigrade oil 10W/40, 10W/50, 15W/50, 20W/40, 20W/50
Ignition distributor shaft, contact-breaker pivot, automatic timing control	Engine oil
Synchromesh gearbox	SAE 80EP
Automatic transmission	Renaultmatic or Mobil ATF 200
Wheel hub bearings	High-melting-point grease

Engine – see Chapter 9

Four-cylinder, water-cooled, push-rod-operated, overhead-valve, in-line units, with clutch and gearbox or automatic transmission mounted behind engine.

Renault workshop manuals and handbooks describe the cars by the model numbers – R1170, R1171, etc. – but owners tend to refer to their cars as (for example) TL and TS models. The relationship is shown by the chart below, which also gives a key to the engine type numbers. Only the UK models are listed.

Model	Vehicle type	Engine type
12L, TL	R1170	810-02
12TN estate, up to August 1972	R1171	810-02
12TN, TL estate – August 1972 on	R1330	810-02
12TS	R1177	810-05
12TR, 12 Auto	R1177	810-06
12TR, TS estate	R1337	810-05

Technical specifications – engine

Capacity	1289 cc (78.66 cu. in.)
Cylinder bore	73 mm (2.874 in.)
Piston stroke	77 mm (3.031 in.)
Compression ratio: 12L, TN	8.5:1
12TL up to October 1975	8.5:1
12TL from October 1975 on	9.5:1
12TR, TS, Auto	9.5:1
Maximum brake-horse power (DIN)	
12L up to October 1975	54 bhp at 5250 rpm
12L from October 1975 on	50 bhp at 5250 rpm
12TL, TN	54 bhp at 5250 rpm
12TS, TR, Auto	60 bhp at 5500 rpm

Engine lubrication, maintenance and repair

Oil grade	See Recommended lubricants, above
Oil filter	Screw-on replaceable canister
Minimum oil pressure: at idling speed	10 lb/sq in. (0.7 kg/cm² or bar)
over 40–50 mph in top gear	50–55 lb/sq in. (3.5–4 kg/cm² or bars)
Valve/rocker clearances: Cold, inlet	0.006 in. (0.15 mm)
exhaust	0.008 in. (0.20 mm)
Hot, inlet	0.007 in. (0.18 mm)
exhaust	0.010 in. (0.25 mm)
Crankshaft end-float	0.002–0.009 in. (0.05–0.23 mm)
Camshaft end-float	0.002–0.005 in. (0.05–0.13 mm)
Cylinder head – maximum bow on seating face for gasket	0.002 in. (0.05 mm)
Gudgeon pin fit	Force fit in connecting rod little end; free turning fit in piston

Torque-wrench settings

	lb ft	Nm
Cylinder-head nuts, engine cold	40–50	55–65
engine hot, within 50 min after being switched off	50	65
Rocker shaft retaining nuts and bolts	10–15	15–17½
Connecting-rod big-end cap nuts	35	45
Main-bearing cap nuts	40–50	55–65
Flywheel fixing bolts: manual transmission	37	50
Converter drive plate: automatic transmission	48–52	65–70

Cooling system – see Chapter 10

Type	Pressurized, sealed system, with expansion bottle. Belt-driven pump and fan
Pressure in system	11½ lb/sq in. (0.8 kg/cm² or bar)
Thermostat opening temperature	86–92°C (187–198°F)
Anti-freeze solution	This must be of a suitable type to prevent corrosion of the engine and heater matrix, and the special Renault coolant should therefore be used

Carburettor and petrol pump – see Chapter 11

Carburettor – 12L, TL, TN	Solex 32 EISA
12TR, TS	Weber 32 DIR21 twin-choke type

Standard jet settings should not be changed without consulting a Renault dealer

Petrol pump	Mechanically operated

Ignition system – see Chapter 12

Firing order	1, 3, 4, 2 (No. 1 cylinder at rear of engine)
Sparking plugs: TL up to October 1975, 12L	AC 43F or Champion L-88A
All other models	AC 42 FS or Champion L-88A
Sparking plug gap	0.025–0.029 in. (0.65–0.75 mm)
Distributor type	Ducellier
Distributor contact-breaker points gap	0.016 in. (0.4 mm)
Dwell – cam angle	57° ± 3°
percentage	63% ± 3

Ignition timing

	Curve	Car model	Static timing
The initial timing setting depends on the automatic advance curve of the distributor. The reference number (eg R.268/C34) is stamped on the of the distributor body or on a clip secured to one of the ignition leads.	R.248/C34	TS	tdc ±1°
	R.251/C34	L, TL up to October 1975	tdc ±1°
	R.268/C34	L, TL up to October 1975	6° ±1°
	R.268/C34	L, after October 1975	tdc ±1°
	R.280/C34	TR, Auto	12° ±1°
	R.280/C52	TL, after October 1975	10° ±1°

Clutch, gearbox and automatic transmission – see Chapter 13

Clutch type release	Diaphragm-spring type, single dry disc with cable-operated

Clutch cable adjustment, free play at end of lever	3/32–9/64 in. (2.5–3.5 mm)

Automatic transmission gearchange speeds (at full throttle kick-down)

The figures are the approximate speeds at which shifts should take place with selector at A or D. Allowance must also be made for possible speedometer error.

1st–2nd, 38 mph   2nd–3rd, 64 mph   3rd–2nd, 57 mph   2nd–1st, 32 mph

Torque-wrench settings

	lb ft	Nm
Syncromesh gearbox		
Clutch assembly to flywheel	35	50
Clutch housing to engine bolts	26-38	35-50
Automatic transmission		
Converter to drive plate fixing bolts	25	35
Converter housing to engine bolts	26-38	35-50

Suspension, steering, tyres – see Chapter 14

The front-wheel alignment and steering geometry checks must be carried out with precision equipment by a Renault dealer. No makeshift adjustments must be made as these may affect the safety and roadholding of the car and may also cause rapid tyre wear.

Torque-wrench settings

Front suspension and steering	lb ft	Nm
Pins – Steering arm	25	35
Front shock absorber bottom fixing	60	80
Nuts – Shock absorber top fixing	10	15
Shock absorber bottom mounting	45	60
Shock absorber bottom fixing lock-nut	45	60
Front anti-roll bar link	10	15
Suspension upper ball joint	35	50
Suspension lower ball joint	35	50
Steering ball joint	25	35
Stub axle	115	160
Road wheel	45–60	60–80
Rack end fitting	30	40
Upper arm castor tie-rod	30	40
Rear suspension		
Pins – Shock absorber lower	20	30
Side arms	25	35
Upper arm	80	110
Upper arm centre bearing	10	15
Centre resilient bush on axle beam	35	50
Brake backplate fixing bolts	30	40
Nuts – Shock absorber top fixing	10	15
Shock absorber bottom fixing	20	30

Tyres

The pressures given below are average figures only. The latest recommendations by the manufacturers of the tyres fitted to your car should always be checked, as there are sometimes variations in the pressures recommended for different makes of tyre. Most garages and tyre specialists should have this information.

Tyre size	Pressures – lb/sq in. (kg/cm² or bars)			
	Normal loads and speeds		Fully laden or high-speed cruising	
	Front	Rear	Front	Rear
Saloon				
145SR-13, 155SR-13, 155HR-13	23 (1.6)	26 (1.8)	26 (1.8)	28 (2.0)
165SR-13	23 (1.6)	27 (1.9)	24 (1.7)	28 (2.0)
Estate car				
155SR-13	23 (1.6)	26 (1.8)	24 (1.7)	28 (2.0)
165SR-13	23 (1.6)	27 (1.9)	24 (1.7)	28 (2.0)

Automatic-transmission models – Increase pressures for front tyres by 2 lb/sq in. (0.1 kg/cm² or bar).

Braking system – see Chapter 15

Hydraulic system, disc brakes at front, drums at rear. Vacuum servo standard on TS, estate and later TL saloon.

Brake fluid   Conforming to SAE J1703 or SAE 70 R3

Torque-wrench settings

Caliper bracket to stub axle carrier fixing bolts, 50 lb ft (65 Nm)

Disc to hub fixing bolts, 15 lb ft (20 Nm)

Stub axle nuts, 115 lb ft (160 Nm)

Brake servo to scuttle fixing nuts, 10 lb ft (13 Nm)

Electrical system – see Chapter 16

12-volt, negative terminal of battery earthed. Alternator fitted as standard.

Weights and measures (approx.)

Overall length – saloon	14 ft 3 in. (4.343 m)
estate	14 ft 5¼ in. (4.400 m)
Overall width	5 ft 4½ in. (1.638 m)
Overall height – saloon	4 ft 8¼ in. (1.435 m)
estate	4 ft 9¼ in. (1.455 m)
Ground clearance, laden	5 in. (127 mm)
Turning circle – saloon	32¾ ft (9.993 m)
estate	35¼ ft (10.744 m)
Weight – L and TL: saloon	16¾ cwt (900 kg)
estate	18¾–19 cwt (950-960 kg)
TS and TR (auto): saloon	18¾ cwt (950 kg)
estate	19¼ cwt (980 kg)

For maximum stability and safety when towing, it is recommended that the loaded weight of a caravan or trailer should not exceed three-quarters of the kerbside weight of the car.

Metric conversion tables

Inches	Decimals	Milli-metres	Inches to millimetres in.	mm	Millimetres to inches mm	in.	°F	°C	°C	°F
1/64	0·015625	0·3969	0·0001	0·00254	0·001	0·000039	−20	−28·9	−30	−22
1/32	0·03125	0·7937	0·0002	0·00508	0·002	0·000079	−15	−26·1	−28	−18·4
3/64	0·046875	1·1906	0·0003	0·00762	0·003	0·000118	−10	−23·3	−26	−14·8
1/16	0·0625	1·5875	0·0004	0·01016	0·004	0·000157	−5	−20·6	−24	−11·2
5/64	0·078125	1·9844	0·0005	0·01270	0·005	0·000197	0	−17·8	−22	−7·6
3/32	0·09375	2·3812	0·0006	0·01524	0·006	0·000236	1	−17·2	−20	−4
7/64	0·109375	2·7781	0·0007	0·01778	0·007	0·000276	2	−16·7	−18	−0·4
1/8	0·125	3·1750	0·0008	0·02032	0·008	0·000315	3	−16·1	−16	3·2
9/64	0·140625	3·5719	0·0009	0·02286	0·009	0·000354	4	−15·6	−14	6·8
5/32	0·15625	3·9687	0·001	0·0254	0·01	0·00039	5	−15·0	−12	10·4
11/64	0·171875	4·3656	0·002	0·0508	0·02	0·00079	10	−12·2	−10	14
3/16	0·1875	4·7625	0·003	0·0762	0·03	0·00118	15	−9·4	−8	17·6
13/64	0·203125	5·1594	0·004	0·1016	0·04	0·00157	20	−6·7	−6	21·2
7/32	0·21875	5·5562	0·005	0·1270	0·05	0·00197	25	−3·9	−4	24·8
15/64	0·234375	5·9531	0·006	0·1524	0·06	0·00236	30	−1·1	−2	28·4
1/4	0·25	6·3500	0·007	0·1778	0·07	0·00276	35	1·7	0	32
17/64	0·265625	6·7469	0·008	0·2032	0·08	0·00315	40	4·4	2	35·6
9/32	0·28125	7·1437	0·009	0·2286	0·09	0·00354	45	7·2	4	39·2
19/64	0·296875	7·5406	0·01	0·254	0·1	0·00394	50	10·0	6	42·8
5/16	0·3125	7·9375	0·02	0·508	0·2	0·00787	55	12·8	8	46·4
21/64	0·328125	8·3344	0·03	0·762	0·3	0·01181	60	15·6	10	50
11/32	0·34375	8·7312	0·04	1·016	0·4	0·01575	65	18·3	12	53·6
23/64	0·359375	9·1281	0·05	1·270	0·5	0·01969	70	21·1	14	57·2
3/8	0·375	9·5250	0·06	1·524	0·6	0·02362	75	23·9	16	60·8
25/64	0·390625	9·9219	0·07	1·778	0·7	0·02756	80	26·7	18	64·4
13/32	0·40625	10·3187	0·08	2·032	0·8	0·03150	85	29·4	20	68
27/64	0·421875	10·7156	0·09	2·286	0·9	0·03543	90	32·2	22	71·6
7/16	0·4375	11·1125	0·1	2·54	1	0·03937	95	35·0	24	75·2
29/64	0·453125	11·5094	0·2	5·08	2	0·07874	100	37·8	26	78·8
15/32	0·46875	11·9062	0·3	7·62	3	0·11811	105	40·6	28	82·4
31/64	0·484375	12·3031	0·4	10·16	4	0·15748	110	43·3	30	86
1/2	0·5	12·7000	0·5	12·70	5	0·19685	115	46·1	32	89·6
33/64	0·515625	13·0969	0·6	15·24	6	0·23622	120	48·9	34	93·2
17/32	0·53125	13·4937	0·7	17·78	7	0·27559	125	51·7	36	96·8
35/64	0·546875	13·8906	0·8	20·32	8	0·31496	130	54·4	38	100·4
9/16	0·5625	14·2875	0·9	22·86	9	0·35433	135	57·2	40	104
37/64	0·578125	14·6844	1	25·4	10	0·39370	140	60·0	42	107·6
19/32	0·59375	15·0812	2	50·8	11	0·43307	145	62·8	44	112·2
39/64	0·609375	15·4781	3	76·2	12	0·47244	150	65·6	46	114·8
5/8	0·625	15·8750	4	101·6	13	0·51181	155	68·3	48	113·4
41/64	0·640625	16·2719	5	127·0	14	0·55118	160	71·1	50	122
21/32	0·65625	16·6687	6	152·4	15	0·59055	165	73·9	52	125·6
43/64	0·67185	17·0656	7	177·8	16	0·62992	170	76·7	54	129·2
11/16	0·6875	17·4625	8	203·2	17	0·66929	175	79·4	56	132·8
45/64	0·703125	17·8594	9	228·6	18	0·70866	180	82·2	58	136·4
23/32	0·71875	18·2562	10	254·0	19	0·74803	185	85·0	60	140
47/64	0·734375	18·6531	11	279·4	20	0·78740	190	87·8	62	143·6
3/4	0·75	19·0500	12	304·8	21	0·82677	195	90·6	64	147·2
49/64	0·765625	19·4469	13	330·2	22	0·86614	200	93·3	66	150·8
25/32	0·78125	19·8437	14	355·6	23	0·90551	205	96·1	68	154·4
51/64	0·796875	20·2406	15	381·0	24	0·94488	210	98·9	70	158
13/16	0·8125	20·6375	16	406·4	25	0·98425	212	100·0	75	167
53/64	0·828125	21·0344	17	431·8	26	1·02362	215	101·7	80	176
27/32	0·84375	21·4312	18	457·2	27	1·06299	220	104·4	85	185
55/64	0·859375	21·8281	19	482·6	28	1·10236	225	107·2	90	194
7/8	0·875	22·2250	20	508·0	29	1·14173	230	110·0	95	203
57/64	0·890625	22·6219	21	533·4	30	1·18110	235	112·8	100	212
29/32	0·90625	23·0187	22	558·8	31	1·22047	240	115·6	105	221
59/64	0·921875	23·4156	23	584·2	32	1·25984	245	118·3	110	230
15/16	0·9375	23·8125	24	609·6	33	1·29921	250	121·1	115	239
61/64	0·953125	24·2094	25	635·0	34	1·33858	255	123·9	120	248
31/32	0·96875	24·6062	26	660·4	35	1·37795	260	126·6	125	257
63/64	0·984375	25·0031	27	690·6	36	1·41732	265	129·4	130	266

How to read the remaining tables in this section

Read the 'tens' in the first or last column and the units along the top. Eg, to convert 25 feet to metres read down to 20 and across to 5 = 7·62 m.

Feet to Metres

(ft)	(m) 0	1	2	3	4	5	6	7	8	9	
—		0·305	0·610	0·914	1·219	1·524	1·829	2·134	2·438	2·743	—
10	3·048	3·353	3·658	3·962	4·267	4·572	4·877	5·182	5·486	5·791	10
20	6·096	6·401	6·706	7·010	7·315	7·620	7·925	8·230	8·534	8·839	20
30	9·144	9·449	9·754	10·058	10·363	10·668	10·973	11·278	11·582	11·887	30
40	12·192	12·497	12·802	13·106	13·411	13·716	14·021	14·326	14·630	14·935	40
50	15·240	15·545	15·850	16·154	16·459	16·764	17·069	17·374	17·678	17·983	50
60	18·288	18·593	18·898	19·202	19·507	19·812	20·117	20·422	20·726	21·031	60
70	21·336	21·641	21·946	22·250	22·555	22·860	23·165	23·470	23·774	24·079	70
80	24·384	24·689	24·994	25·298	25·603	25·908	26·213	26·518	26·822	27·127	80
90	27·432	27·737	28·042	28·346	28·651	28·956	29·261	29·566	29·870	30·175	90

Square Inches to Square Centimetres

(sq. in. or in.²)	(cm²) 0	1	2	3	4	5	6	7	8	9	
—		6·452	12·903	19·355	25·807	32·258	38·710	45·161	51·613	58·065	—
10	64·516	70·968	70·420	83·871	90·323	96·774	103·226	109·678	116·129	122·581	10
20	129·033	135·484	141·936	148·387	154·839	161·291	167·742	174·194	180·646	187·097	20
30	193·549	200·000	206·452	212·904	219·355	225·807	232·259	238·710	245·162	251·613	30
40	258·065	264·517	270·968	277·420	283·871	290·323	296·775	303·226	309·678	316·130	40
50	322·581	329·033	335·485	341·936	348·388	354·839	361·291	367·743	374·194	380·646	50
60	387·098	393·549	400·001	406·452	412·904	419·356	425·807	432·259	438·711	445·162	60
70	451·614	458·065	464·517	470·969	477·420	483·872	490·324	496·775	503·227	509·678	70
80	516·130	522·582	529·033	535·485	541·937	548·388	554·840	561·291	567·743	574·195	80
90	580·646	587·099	593·550	600·001	606·453	612·904	619·356	625·808	632·259	638·711	90

Cubic Inches to Cubic Centimetres

(cu in. or in³)	(cc or cm³) 0	1	2	3	4	5	6	7	8	9	
—		16·387	32·774	49·162	65·549	81·936	98·323	114·710	131·097	147·484	—
10	163·872	180·259	196·646	213·033	229·420	245·808	262·195	278·582	294·969	311·356	10
20	327·743	344·130	360·518	376·905	393·292	409·679	426·066	442·453	458·841	475·228	20
30	491·615	508·002	524·389	540·776	557·164	573·551	589·938	606·325	622·712	639·099	30
40	655·486	671·874	688·261	704·648	721·035	737·422	753·809	770·197	786·584	802·971	40
50	819·358	835·745	852·132	868·520	884·907	901·294	917·681	934·068	950·455	966·843	50
60	983·230	999·617	1016·004	1032·391	1048·778	1065·166	1081·553	1097·940	1114·327	1130·714	60
70	1147·101	1163·489	1179·876	1196·263	1212·650	1229·037	1245·424	1261·811	1278·199	1294·586	70
80	1310·973	1327·360	1343·747	1360·134	1376·522	1392·909	1409·296	1425·683	1442·070	1458·457	80
90	1474·845	1491·232	1507·619	1524·006	1540·393	1556·780	1573·168	1589·555	1605·942	1622·329	90

Pounds to Kilogrammes

(lb)	(kg) 0	1	2	3	4	5	6	7	8	9	
—		0·454	0·907	1·361	1·814	2·268	2·722	3·175	3·629	4·082	—
10	4·536	4·990	5·443	5·897	6·350	6·804	7·257	7·711	8·165	8·618	10
20	9·072	9·525	9·979	10·433	10·886	11·340	11·793	12·247	12·701	13·154	20
30	13·608	14·061	14·515	14·968	15·422	15·876	16·329	16·783	17·237	17·690	30
40	18·144	18·597	19·051	19·504	19·958	20·412	20·865	21·319	21·772	22·226	40
50	22·680	23·133	23·587	24·040	24·494	24·948	25·401	25·855	26·308	26·762	50
60	27·216	27·669	28·123	28·576	29·030	29·484	29·937	30·391	30·844	31·298	60
70	31·751	32·205	32·659	33·112	33·566	34·019	34·473	34·927	35·380	35·834	70
80	36·287	36·741	37·195	37·648	38·102	38·855	39·009	39·463	39·916	40·370	80
90	40·823	41·277	41·731	42·184	42·638	43·091	43·545	43·998	44·452	44·906	90

ndex

Accelerator cable, kick-down adjustment, 74
Air filter, 24, 61
Alternator, 35
  belt, 57
  faults, 29
  servicing, 97
  testing, 102
Anti-freeze solutions, 55
Automatic transmission, 8, 11, 69, 73, 106
  adjustments, 74, 75
  capacity, 104
  draining and refilling, 73
  oil level, 73
  overhauls, 69
  removing and refitting, 75
  starter inhibitor switch, 75
  torque converter, 51, 52, 69, 75

Balancing wheels, 79
Battery, 96
  charge indicator, 97
  servicing and topping, 96
Bodywork, 10, 30, 34
Braking system, 9, 11, 12, 33, 86
  adjustments, 88
  bleeding, 87
  caliper, removing, 92
  disc brakes, 91–92
  drum brakes, 89, 90
  faults, 11, 12, 33
  fluid, 12, 33, 87, 108
  handbrake, adjusting, 88
  hoses, 12
  pads, 91
  pressure-drop bypass unit, 94
  pressure-drop indicator, 94
  pressure-limiting valve, 86, 93
  servo, 86, 95
  shoes, fitting, 89, 90
  stop lamp, 101
  topping-up reservoir, 87
Buying a used car, 10

Camshaft, 46, 105
  chain and sprockets, 45
Capacities, oil, petrol, water, 104
Carburettor, 59, 106
  acceleration pump, 61
  adjustment, 59–60
  air filter, 24, 61
  de-fuming valve, 61
  emission-controlled types, 62
  faults, 24
  filter, 61
  float chamber and float, 60
  jets, 60, 61

  needle valve, 61
  servicing, 60–61
Clutch, 11, 35, 69
  adjusting, 69, 106
  cable, 71
  faults, 25, 70
  overhauls, 70
  withdrawal bearing, 71
Compression ratio, 105
Connecting rods 36, 50
  bearings, 50
Contact-breaker, 66
  adjustment, 66
  dwell angle, 106
  gap, 66, 106
  removing and refitting, 66
Cooling system, 54, 106
  anti-freeze, 55
  belt adjustment, 57
  capacity, 104
  draining, 56
  expansion bottle valve, 54, 56, 106
  faults, 22
  flushing, 56
  leaks, 54
  overheating, 22
  radiator, 58
  thermostat, 57, 106
  topping-up, 54
  water capacity, 104
  water pump, 57
Crankcase ventilation, 40
Crankshaft, bearings and oil seals, 36, 51, 105
Cylinder barrels, 35–36, 41, 50
Cylinder head, 8, 105
  decarbonizing, 42
  dismantling, 41
  gasket, 40, 44
  removing, 8, 40
  replacing, 44

Decarbonizing, 40, 42, 44
Dimensions, 108
Direction indicators, 33, 101
Disc brakes, 91–92
  caliper, 92
  renewing pads, 91
Distributor, ignition, 64, 66
  cap, 64, 65
  contacts, 66
  dismantling and reassembling, 66
  driving shaft, 49
  lubrication, 64
  removing and refitting, 66
  rotor, 65
  testing, 65

Drive shafts, 11, 76
  removing and refitting, 76
Drum brakes, 89, 90

Electrical system —
  alternator, 29, 97, 102
  battery, 96
  battery maintenance, 96, 97
  direction indicators, 33, 101
  faults, 29
  fuses, 101
  lamps, 34, 99, 100
  specifications, 105
  starter motor, 97
  windscreen wiper and washer, 100
  wiring diagrams, 103
Engine, 8, 10, 11, 37
  changing oil, 37
  compression ratio, 105
  crankcase ventilation system, 40
  decarbonizing, 40, 42
  faults, 20, 21
  firing order, 106
  lubrication, 37, 105
  oil filter, 38
  oil pressure, 37, 105
  oil-pressure relief valve, 49
  oil pump, 49
  oil sump, 37
  overhauls, 35, 40
  power output, 105
  refitting, 52, 53
  removing, 52, 53
  specification, 105
  timing, 67, 68, 106
  timing chain, 45
  top-overhaul, 40
  tune-up, 19
  turning when making adjustments, 16
Exhaust system, 12

Fan-belt, tensioning, 57
Fault-tracing charts, 20–29
Firing order, 106
Flywheel, 51, 52
Front suspension, 79
front-wheel alignment, 79, 85
Fuel consumption, 9
Fuel grade, 104
Fuel pump — see Petrol pump
Fuses, 101

Gearbox, 8, 11, 72
  capacity, 104
  draining and refilling, 72, 104
  faults, 11, 25
  oil level, 72
  oil seal, 71

overhauls, 69
removing and refitting, 72
Grinding-in valves, 42
Gudgeon pins, 50

Handbrake, 88
Headlamps —
renewing bulbs or light units, 99
setting, 100
High-tension leads, 63

Idling adjustments, 59–60
Ignition system, 63, 106
capacitor, 64
coil, 63
contact-breaker, 66
distributor, 64
faults, 23
firing order, 106
leads, 63
sparking plugs, 63, 106
timing, 65, 67–68, 106
vacuum timing control, 65
Instrument panel lights, 100

Jets, carburettor, 60, 61

Lights, 33, 34, 99, 100
Lubricants, recommended, 105

Main bearings, 51
Maintenance schedule, 12–15
Manifolds, 42
Ministry test, 33

Oil —
changing, engine, 37, 104
gearbox, 72, 104
automatic transmission, 73
filter, 38
pressure, 37, 105
pump, 49
recommended grades, 105
sump, 37, 47
Overheating, 22

Panel and warning lamps, 100
Performance figures, 9, 10
Petrol —
consumption, 9
recommended grades, 104
Petrol tank capacity, 104
Petrol pump, 61
cleaning filter, 62
faults, 24, 62

Piston rings, 35–36
Pistons, 35–36, 44, 50
Push-rods, 41, 47

Radiator —
expansion-bottle valve pressure, 56, 106
removing, 58
topping-up, 54
water capacity, 104
Rear lights, 100
Rear suspension, 82
Rear-wheel bearings, 83
Relining brakes, 89, 90
Road tests, 9, 10
Rocker shaft, 42
Routine maintenance, 12–15

Seat belts, 34
Servicing, routine, 12–15
Servo, braking system, 86, 95
Shock absorbers, 79, 82
Side lamps, 100
Slow-running adjustments, 59–60
Sparking plugs, 20, 63
cleaning and setting, 63
faults, 20
gaps, 63, 106
leads, 63
suitable types, 63, 106
Specifications, 9, 104–108
Springs, 82
Starter motor, 97
removing and refitting, 98
servicing, 97
Starting troubles, 20
Steering gear, 8, 9, 34, 84
adjustment, 79, 85
alignment, 79, 85
ball joints, 34, 85
faults, 11, 27, 34, 85
rack, removing and refitting, 85
repairs, 85
Stop lamp, 33, 101
Sump oil, 37
Suspension, 8, 9, 11
ball joints, 79, 80
coil springs, 82
dampers, 79, 82
faults, 11, 26
front, 79
overhauls, 80–84
rear, 82
shock absorbers, 79
stub-axle carrier, 80

Tappet clearances, 38, 105
Tappets, 46, 47
Thermostat, 57, 106
Timing chain and sprockets, 45
Timing chain tensioner, 45, 46
Timing cover oil seal, 44
Timing ignition, 67–68, 106
Tools, 16
Top-overhaul, 40
Topping-up —
battery, 96
brake reservoir, 87
cooling system, 54
Torque converter, 51, 52, 69, 75
Torque-wrench figures, 106, 107, 108
Transmission — see clutch, gearbox
automatic transmission, drive shafts
Tyres, 34
faults, 12, 34
pressure gauge, 16
pressures, 108
size, 108
tread-depth gauge, 16
wear, 16, 79

Universal joints, 11, 76

Vacuum —
servo, 86, 95
timing control, 65
Valves, 38
clearances, 38, 105
grinding, 42
guides, 42
reassembling, 43
removing, 42
rockers, 38, 42
seating, 42
springs, 42, 43
tappets, 46, 47

Water capacity, 104
Water pump, 57
Weights, 108
Wheels —
alignment, 79, 85
balance, 79
bearings, 11, 80
wheel-wobble, 79
Windscreen washer, 33, 100
Windscreen wiper, 100
Wiring diagram, 103